THE BOOK OF HAT

AT HAT'S WISH
$1
FROM EVERY BOOK
SOLD WILL BE
DONATED TO

canTeen
Supporting young people
living with cancer
canteen.org.nz

THE BOOK OF HAT

HARRIET ROWLAND

Mākaro Press thanks Fifi Colston for her cover, Stefanie Hester & Jan Kelly for proofreading, Ian Stewart & Andrew Matangi for legal advice, Sharon Exley & team at Wakefields Digital for Harriet's special copy of *The Book of Hat*.

First published 2014

ISBN 978-0-473-27285-2
A catalogue record for this book is available from the National Library of New Zealand

Cover image: Fifi Colston
Cover design: Fifi Colston with Matthew Bartlett
Book design & typesetting: Paul Stewart
Editor: Mary McCallum
Printed by Printstop, Wellington, NZ

Submarine books
Mākaro Press PO Box 41-032 Eastbourne 5047
makaropress@gmail.com makaropress.wordpress.com

Harriet Rowland — known as Hat — was 17 when she was diagnosed with osteosarcoma, a rare form of cancer that began in her knee. At the time she was a student at Queen Margaret College in Wellington, New Zealand.

Going through treatment was often a lonely time, as friends — while supportive — didn't always understand Hat's new life. This was until she fell in love with the character Hazel Grace from John Green's novel *The Fault in Our Stars*, a girl who talks honestly and openly about living with cancer. Like her, Hat found life changed in ways that were both good and bad: falling in love and hospital stays among them. And she was surprised by how much happiness there was still to find.

Throughout her journey, Hat has kept a blog called *My Experience of Walking the Dog*, and this book is a collection of those posts edited with the author. Why the blog title? Her parents say cancer is like a dog — fine if it stays in its own yard. Hat's dog got out. This is her unexpected story.

MYEXPERIENCEOFWALKINGTHEDOG.BLOGSPOT.CO.NZ

To those who have danced through the storm
with me, there will never be enough
thank yous and I love yous for me to give.
We may be bruised and a bit battered
but I wouldn't change any of you one bit.
You truly are my own personal miracle.

'Keep your shit together,' I whispered to my lungs.
The Fault in Our Stars by John Green

FROM HAT

Life is a strange thing. It never seems to work out how you think it will. You can dream about the future, imagine what it will be like, but life has this naughty way of being, 'I don't *think* so!' Life is constantly changing, and I guess we all learn how to adapt and change too. Nothing is certain when it comes to the future. Apart from death. Everybody has to die.

I was thinking about this the other day. The people who have met me since I've had cancer sometimes find it hard to fathom what I used to be like. The changes are not always for the better, but in my case I like who I am now as a person. I miss being the 10 kgs lighter that I used to be, but you can't have everything — even though I try to! I had to grow up quickly with this illness, and I wouldn't change anything about that.

The truth is, if I hadn't been through it all, I wouldn't be who I am today. Dog or no dog.

SUNDAY, 28 AUGUST 2011

LIFE IS MOST DEFINITELY LIKE A ROLLER COASTER

I DON'T KNOW WHETHER TO LAUGH OR CRY when I think about the mess I am in. I don't know what is going to happen, whether I will grow old, whether I will graduate from high school or university. Life wasn't supposed to be like this. I am 17 years old, my biggest worry in life should be that my parents won't give me enough money for ball dresses, or stressing about due dates for homework. I should not be sitting here wondering whether I have cancer or not.

I hate that the doctors won't tell me, and my dad won't tell me. I want to believe that I am fine, but I have a tumour growing inside me and everyone is tiptoeing around smiling that same sad smile. They tell me they love me, but I don't understand what is going on. I want to be strong. I need to be strong. I try to smile and act nonchalant about it. Smile, laugh and act like it doesn't bother me. I can't focus. I just want to understand what is going to happen to me.

On Monday, I was a normal teenager. I went to hospital because my knee was sore after skiing. I thought my ligament had torn … how wrong was I!

I have a lesion on my left knee. I have since had two X-rays and a blood test, which I found out I hate! (I don't think the nurse was impressed when I chucked into the sink.) I have had a CT and an MRI and a bone scan. It's my birthday on Friday, I am going to be 18. This was supposed to be the start of my adult life but I don't want to start it like this. I want to be healthy, not trying to figure out whether I can get into university or not and if I will miss school. I wish I had never gone to the doctor. I wish I was still ignorant.

I WROTE THIS ON WEDNESDAY,
AND A LOT HAS CHANGED SINCE THEN ...

I found out that I do have cancer. I have a tumour growing within the femur in my left knee. In some sense, I don't think it has hit me that I have cancer because I cannot stop laughing. The situation is hilarious! I almost feel like my life is like a movie because it is sooo overly dramatic — none of it feels real. In one week, my brother cut his median nerve and tendon (the main ones to his left hand) and is now exhibiting THE CLAW! Then I got told on Thursday that I have cancer. Friday, ironically, was the Cancer Society's Daffodil Day and my eighteenth birthday! If only my life had theme music. And I wonder, if my life is a movie, how will it end?

My family says having cancer is like having a dog, because as long as it stays in its yard it's okay. When it starts digging up the bushes in the neighbour's garden … not so much! I have started to tell some of my friends. This is easily one of the hardest things I have had to do. How do you say 'I have cancer' in a good or easy way? If anyone has any ideas please tell me, as I am shocking at it! I watch people try to figure out if I'm being serious, and when they realise I am, I have to watch the emotions course across their faces. If they start crying, my heart breaks a little. I want to say sorry (and often do) because all I want to do is fix it.

Tomorrow, I am going to Auckland to see a specialist. To find out more by doing a biopsy. This scares me as I don't know what they will find, or if I will like what they find.

MONDAY, 29 AUGUST 2011

TOMORROW IS WHEN THE WAR BEGINS

TOMORROW WILL BE THE FIRST DAY OF THE REST OF MY LIFE. I am Harriet Rowland and tomorrow I start my battle. The battle to beat my own personal dog. Osteosarcoma. This is my mission and, considering how many times my phone has gone off, I have a support crew that could fill a stadium.

Today I went to school. This in itself is strange, but not because I am some rebellious child and wag all the time. It is strange because school seems so unimportant and insignificant now. What really matters are my friends and family, and spending as much time as I can with them.

Today I flew to Auckland. My parents and my brother are fussing over me. I am in a private room (which I am told is a very good thing). However, the curtains are mustard and the toilet has a nana seat over it. Overall I would give this accommodation a three out of ten. It is odd at night, though. It's not quiet as there are constant sounds, yet there is this airy quietness that permeates the whole hospital. I feel like I am trapped in an old folks' home! The thing about being here (with no wifi!!!) is the isolation. The fact that I mention 'isolation' means I have definitely been at school for far too long. I observe this room, and the thing that I notice is the bed is alone in the centre of the room. If my life is indeed like a movie, this shot would be examined as portraying isolation.

Today I found out I might never ski again. This may not sound like much to some people, but skiing is one of the most important things to me. It's something I have done with my family for my entire life. It's one thing I am good at. It makes me happy. No. It makes me elated. Nothing beats the rush of that first drop or the wind slapping your face. On a side note, I might also become infertile.

WEDNESDAY, 31 AUGUST 2011

FOUR IN A MILLION

I AM ONE OF FOUR PEOPLE IN EVERY MILLION that is diagnosed with osteosarcoma. Consequently, whenever the doctors come to see me there are millions of them! I almost feel like I am some sort of exciting new toy. I guess, when you consider how rare this is, I am indeed the doctors' own personal sparkly toy.

Yesterday I had the biopsy. It was a rather strange experience. To start with, there was a man across the room waiting in the pre-op bay who had nasty scabs all up and down his arms, and looked like somebody you'd cross the road to avoid. Then I was wheeled into the theatre — a strange feeling in itself. You are pushed on your back and you are still, but the world is moving around you. The nurse gave me an injection and told me to breathe in and out of one of those masks and count … 1 … 2 … 3 … 4 … 5 … 6 … 7 … 8 … 9 … 10 …

When I woke up, I was back in my room yet I was *so* not there! It felt like I was sitting above my bed watching the conversations that surrounded me. I felt like I was becoming old. I could not stay awake. Half way through a conversation my head would droop … and … and …

I woke up at 1:30 am needing to pee, and I had three nurses help me get to the bathroom because I had to keep my leg straight — it hurt too much to bend. I had to have the nana toilet seat, and when they rolled me into the bathroom my nausea successfully made me throw up what little was left of my stomach contents. After more pain relief and anti-nausea medication, I went back to play with the fairies …

I woke up later in the morning feeling much better. The drugs had worn off and I was able to stomach some breakfast. Lunch was a different matter, it really looked like sick on a plate so Father was kind and got me some sushi :)

I found out the plan for the next two years of my life. I am going to have chemotherapy for the next twelve weeks, then have the tumour removed and part of my knee replaced. I will have chemotherapy for another six to twelve months.

I am going back to Wellington tomorrow. This makes me sooo happy. It's lonely here. The flowers my friend Hannah sent and the cards from my friends and family make it bearable, but when I was told that I might stay here for the chemo, I almost broke down. I have accepted that I have cancer and that I need to fight it, but the idea of leaving my friends would be too hard. They are a big part of my life and bring me so much happiness, and always will.

THURSDAY, 1 SEPTEMBER 2011

WELCOME HOME

HOME IS MOST CERTAINLY WHERE THE HEART IS and my heart is in Wellington. As the plane slowly descended to this great city of ours, I could not suppress the smile that jumped to my face. This smile only widened as I got off the plane and saw three of my amazing friends waiting for me at the gate. They made me realise how lucky I am in so many ways! And a stream of friends came to see me when I arrived home this afternoon.

Things like this also make you realise who your great friends are, and who are not. Today I heard about a girl who had broken down crying saying, 'My best friend has cancer.' I was slightly bewildered by this. A girl I would consider an acquaintance, who I don't think has my cell phone number, is suddenly calling me her 'best friend'.

At first I thought it was slightly degrading, but I had a wee chuckle, and then I realised something. This is a big deal for so many of the people I know. Nearly everyone I know has been affected by cancer: an aunt, an uncle, a family friend ... they have all suffered from it. The difference for me, though, is that

I am a mere 18 years old and still at school. My life has barely begun. This scares people as it breaks apart the idea that teenagers are indestructible. It shows we are every bit as human as everyone else.

SUNDAY, 4 SEPTEMBER 2011

THE DILEMMA

IT'S A WEIRD IDEA. I never thought my life would end up being like this, but strangely I never could imagine my life after school. School is all I have ever known — it has been my life. Or a large part of my life at least. I have been on this earth 18 years. I have attended school for the better two-thirds of my life. The first third hardly counts because I was so small!

I remember last year there was a group on Facebook saying, 'If the world ends in 2012, I've wasted my whole life in school … lovely.' At the time I had a chuckle, but if my life was to end now I would have spent my *entire* life in school. I do not think this is fair.

I have decided to live my life to the fullest — not that I didn't before! (Ask anyone who took IB with me in year 12 and they shall tell you so.) My eyes have been opened to how much time I have on this earth, and I remind you to appreciate what you have and live in the present.

My dad would always tell me when I asked questions about what came next, 'Just live in the moment!' This used to frustrate me because I always wanted to know what I was doing next!!! But, as usual, he was right. We should just enjoy today, and enjoy tomorrow when it comes.

This is my roundabout way of explaining why I have not blogged for the past couple of days.

My leg is slowly coming right since the biopsy. I hope that by the time the Scots' ball comes around (in eleven days!!!) I should be back to how I was before the surgery. The school balls are my escape. I am not the most girly of girls but I love balls. I love dressing up. Whether it is as a cowboy or a pirate or a princess, I simply adore it. I love the pretence, fantasy and magic around balls. This year I have gone to two, and I have another two to go.

There is only one slight problem … I am getting a Hickman line inserted on Friday. This is to put the chemotherapy and any other medication into my body. It is important that the drugs go into a vein, but when the doctors say they have an antidote on hand you wonder whether they are trying to kill you! However, off topic as normal, the Hickman line is a thin plastic tube that goes through my chest. How are you supposed to look good at a ball when you have a piece of plastic sticking out of your chest?!?

MONDAY, 5 SEPTEMBER 2011

I WISH I WAS PREGNANT ...

WHEN THE GIRLS AT MY SCHOOL found out something was wrong with me, they were unsure what it was. Many hypotheses flew around school. However, the most popular train of thought led the majority of girls to conclude I was probably pregnant. I wish that had been true ...

Today has been soul shattering. I spent eight hours trawling around the hospital being prodded, pricked and even probed like some alien experiment. I had my blood taken four times, became radioactive and got told I have excellent hearing.

I wonder how these doctors and nurses see me. Apart from having a limp and almost fainting when they tried to rob me of my blood, I show no obvious signs of being sick. I have no physical markers to show there is something insanely wrong with my body, and I guess that's what is so odd. It seemed like such a little thing — I thought I had torn a tendon. It never crossed my mind that I would have cancer.

Back to my train of thought: what will these doctors think when they see my chart? They must see millions of people going through the hospital everyday …

Hospitals are strange things, they give you this false sense that the majority of people face life-threatening illnesses. I wonder if the people in hospital sometimes feel like they are the privileged ones instead of the healthy. This would be an awesome way to view the world. The idea that *everyone* is facing illnesses is comforting, however false. It makes you feel as if you are not alone.

I am different from most people I know.

While many people choose to be different with alternative ideas or fashion statements, I am different, but *not* by choice. I am different because of this ridiculous thing growing inside me. I never gave it permission to be there! It's my body — *I* should decide what goes in and out. I guess I still want to believe I am in charge.

I am so unbelievably mad at cancer. I was doing well in school! I was getting above-average marks! I had plans to go to Rhythm and Vines over summer and then to Venture (a ten-day outdoor pursuit sort of camp in Tasmania). I was going to go to Otago next year and now … my life is fighting this.

I HAD NO CHOICE.

THAT IS THE HARDEST PART.

THURSDAY, 8 SEPTEMBER 2011

THE FROOT LOOP SITUATION

So tomorrow I am having my Hickman line put in. I have to be at the hospital at 7am. Now this is purely ridiculous. What sane teenager is out of bed before ten? Most don't even realise the sun is shining before midday. I think someone should create a system so the older you are the earlier your surgery, and go backwards from there.

It's weird because I have been thinking about what is going to happen next year. My cancerous status has almost become old news to many. This treatment is going to take well over a year, and I wonder who will be with me at the end of it, because a year is a long time. People change and move on. They will begin new lives next year and set off into the world.

I wonder how many will keep in contact. This is a serious issue as I am absolutely useless at texting back, Facebooking or emailing. Any sort of reply may take hours, months, years! If you are unlucky, it might not even happen at all … Now this is not because I don't love you. One of my best mates said to me tonight, 'I like it when you don't reply, it reinforces the fact that I'm talking to Harriet Rowland.' I do appreciate every email, text, call and visit, as this is my contact with the human world. As my friends know, I am just one Froot Loop away from being called insane. My support crowd is what gives me some perspective on the real world … and gossip :)

But in all seriousness, friends are the things that keep you going. Messages remind me that I am not getting left behind. Texts remind me how loved I am. Facebook reminds me of the power of procrastination. Calls and visits keep me sane.

I do not intend becoming an odd child whose life is cancer. I intend to be *me* until the end.

I THANK MY SUPPORTIVE
FRIENDS AND FAMILY
FOR NOT PASSING ME
THAT LAST FROOT LOOP.

FRIDAY, 9 SEPTEMBER 2011

ALL I WANT FOR CHRISTMAS IS TO BE NORMAL

THE HICKMAN LINE IS A GO! It is such a strange thing. I have had two cuts made. One is where the dangly bits come out. The surgeon was awesome, so there is no chance that it's going to be showing at either school ball! I will look like a normal 18 year old — though this meant that I had a room of people looking at me topless for well over an hour. I really wish I *was* normal …

The other slit is on the right side of my body, just above the clavicle. I was actually so impressed my year 11 PE came in handy today!! I know what a clavicle is!!! I felt pretty smart when I didn't need the surgeon to explain what it was.

The Hickman line is painful, but strangely not where the dangly bits hang out. It hurts on the other side, but it's okay if I restrict movement of my upper body. So I was thinking, Mum and Dad, it's a bit too hard for me to do chores at the moment …

My family has been awesome throughout all of this. My brother is a little miffed, still, at how he only got one day of glory over his torn median nerve and tendon because I got told the next day that it was likely I had cancer. Sorry and better luck next time, bro.

My mum was waiting for me after my surgery. Once I had come back from the general anaesthetic (sort of) they wheeled me to see her. She was sooo happy to see me!! But then they had to start checking the incisions, and all of a sudden she felt nauseated. Of course, being my mother, she jumps onto my bed and is suddenly the patient, and the nurse frets over her wanting to take her blood pressure.

That's the thing for me, I have to laugh at all this. I think I have developed a really black sort of humour out of necessity. The only other thing I could do is cry because life is so unfair.

As soon as it was announced that the Rugby World Cup was going to be in New Zealand, and I realised I was going to be 18, I have dreamed about it! When the tickets came out, Dad brought two tickets to every game so my brother and I could go to about half each. I am a born and bred kiwi. I love my rugby. After the last Rugby World Cup, I was so disappointed I could not bring myself to watch another game for months.

Originally I had planned on watching the opening ceremony with my friends in town, but I had surgery today, so I just watched it at home with my parents. As the ceremony unfolded, I realised I might not be lucid enough to watch the final live on TV. I almost cried with the unfairness of it.

The thing you need to know about me is I don't cry. I have only cried twice because of this cancer. Once was to my friend out of sheer frustration at the fact that my parents would not tell me what was going on, and the other time was to my dean at school.

My dean is one of the most amazing women alive. She is strong and hilariously funny. All girls who have been in year 13 at Queen Margaret College over the past years will understand. This woman is a living legend. She is wise, kind, understanding and listens to your point of view no matter what.

However, on the day I found out, I decided to go back to school for the afternoon. As I was walking to Hobby (my common room), I saw her and all the feelings racing around inside me resulted in tears leaking from my eyes without permission. That was two weeks ago.

I actually hate this. I hate the fact that I have to be strong. I hate that this is thrust on me. I hate the unfairness of it.

SO MY WISH LIST HAS NOW CHANGED ...
I NO LONGER WISH FOR A PERFECT LIFE.
I WISH FOR A NORMAL ONE.
IS THAT TOO MUCH TO ASK?

MONDAY, 12 SEPTEMBER 2011

BLAST OFF IN 10 ... 9 ... 8 ... ...

I FEEL LIKE A CAN OF WORMS. The nerves have slowly started setting in all day. I realise that in less than twelve hours I am going to be starting chemotherapy. This is the beginning — the beginning of my new life. My old life was full of childlike fun, and occasionally some work. Usually not. Today, my new life will begin. It will be full of white, sterile floors, tubes and — worst of all — fear.

The fear is the thing that nobody wants to face. Up until now I could pretend it was not actually happening. I felt fine. Cancer was almost an abstract idea — one that was true, but not. Now I have no choice. I have to face the fact that it's real, and I am about to get really sick.

There is one thing that nobody ever mentions: I may not survive this. There is a 70% chance I will, but that still leaves a 30% chance that I won't. I don't want to think about what will happen if I am in that 30%, and that is why nobody wants to mention it, because nobody knows what they will do.

Emma is forever saying, 'You should stop trying to please people because you can't please everyone.' But you know what? For once my approach may be an advantage because I have no intention whatsoever of making people sad. I am going to fight this with everything I have. This sounds clichéd, but I really think it can eat my shorts!!! I am going nowhere.

This is a massive mountain, and tomorrow will be the beginning of it. The doctors are going to try to kill me as much as they can without actually killing me … not sure my body is going to be very pleased with this idea.

Not just for one month or a couple of weeks but for over a year, I am going to be pushed as far as I can go. I am going to be run over with tractors and lawnmowers, dragged behind the ferry and thrown from twenty-foot buildings in an attempt to make me well.

It's an odd concept as I don't feel sick — you see me and nothing seems wrong. I have tubes sticking out, which are a bit sore, and my knees are not always happy with me, but apart from that I am a fit 18-year-old girl. All my tests say I am in good condition except for one nasty dog bite.

That dog bite is going to go away. I am going to get better because this is my life and I intend to be here for a long time.

MONDAY, 12 SEPTEMBER 2011

THE GLORY OF HOSPITALS

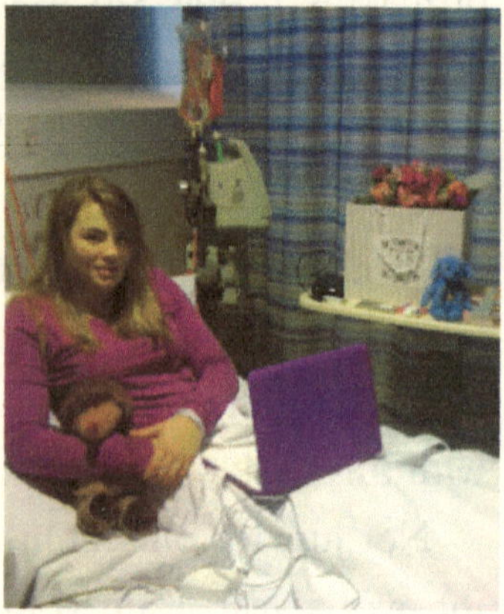

OKAY. THIS IS NOWHERE NEAR AS FRIGHTENING as I thought it would be. I feel fine. All I am doing is peeing like there is no tomorrow! Then again I have only just started.

The list they read us of the possible side effects of chemo sounded rather dire. Not something I really want to think about.

I felt so lovely when I walked into the ward and there were some flowers waiting for me from good family friends. Support makes this so much easier. I was put in a room with a doddery old woman called Dolores who promptly excreted into her bed. Joyous, right?

I do, however, have the pleasure of visitors and, in a place like this, I *love* visitors. I always have, but here more so, since the closest people to my age are worrying more about menopause and less about uni next year.

I wonder if I will feel different later as I have only been getting chemo for less than an hour, and bucketloads of fluids before that. Oh well, whatever happens, onwards march!!!

TUESDAY, 13 SEPTEMBER 2011

DAY 2

FEELING: PRETTY AVERAGE. Wish: to have a new room-mate (she wet the bed last night and pees in a bed pan, need I say more). I have now received nearly all of the chemo, and they are just keeping me in under observation. Hearing the possible side effects is not an experience I recommend for anybody. I like ignorance, I think.

My body is feeling odd. I don't feel sick exactly but I have waves of nausea coming and going. They are not very nice, and usually come when I am standing up and moving around. I don't feel like eating much at all. I am lucky I am able to receive anti-nausea medicine and lots of it!

I have a weird tingly sensation in my toes and fingers, which I have been told is a common side effect. It's strange, like non-painful pins and needles. I can't really describe it. I am tired all the time, but that was expected.

I had friends over yesterday after school and, as my room-mate had kindly left a present in her bed, we went to this amazing CanTeen room. We played rounds of video games! It was so grand because I managed to forget that I was in hospital. We had such a fun afternoon. People coming to visit actually make the place much more bearable.

My mother! Of course! She must be a subject at some point even though I can imagine her *gosh* sigh already. Yesterday when we were being told the side effects, she decided she couldn't take me being the patient anymore and leaned back so quickly she banged her head against the wall! She is the biggest clutz out.

But I do love her, she has been great. She's so strong and I really admire her for it. This is one of those situations you never want to be in. Your child has cancer. This must be a fear that crosses all new and old parents' minds. I am so sorry you have to go through this, Mum, but I love your strength.

I think I might have to stop now, the room is starting to smell a bit funky again. If I get that decrepit, please shoot me.

THURSDAY, 22 SEPTEMBER 2011

THE QUESTION OF THE TURD

WELL ... THAT SUCKED. Walking the dog is not as pleasant as it sounds. It has been a rough week. It was strange, though, because when I first went into hospital I was fine. The chemo started and I was fine ... but I got progressively sicker and sicker.

I couldn't eat anything, and fluids were administered through my Hickman line for three days after my chemo finished. I am supposed to drink at least two litres of fluid a day, so I am like a yo-yo between bed and the toilet!

Those who visited me got very used to the frequent visits to the toilet, and I must thank them for that. Visitors — whether they are young or old, close or not — are wonderful. I really appreciated everyone who came and saw me. It was a great distraction talking to people or, in many cases, listening to the conversation surrounding me.

The other thing that has been awesome has been the number of letters and cards and Facebook messages and texts from people constantly reminding me that they are there for me. It sounds weird, but it's easier walking the dog with people who care.

Today, I went and got a wig from this amazing lady who lives in Northland. I went to her house and sat and chose my wig (and did some serious damage on the parental wallet), but what struck me was how lucky I am.

Don't get me wrong, I understand I have absolutely terrible luck to be the one person in the entire Wellington region (statistically) to be diagnosed with osteosarcoma this year. But I am lucky in the fact that I have amazing parents and friends, and a support system I would find hard to rival.

My mum has been allowed to take the rest of this year off to look after me. This is sooo fortunate. I am extremely lucky that we are able to do this. Thank you, parents, for not flunking out of uni and working hard!

This is really good for me because I have been relegated to baby status this past week. In hospital I even had to have my mum help me have a shower. I was completely useless. I could not text, go on Facebook, read, even watch TV. I was a complete invalid.

I am happy to be home and feeling better, finally. I had to have a complete change of anti-nausea drug regime from the first one I was on, and it is now about a week since chemotherapy finished, but I am feeling much better.

So now the question of the turd — a metaphorical one, not a real one this time. I am at the stage where I have to wonder whether I am still nauseous because of the chemo or nauseous because of the continuous drugs. Ten pills a day does not keep the doctor away… unfortunately. So the plan is to slowly ween myself off my drug habit.

This post has been written over two days so please excuse the disjointedness of some of it. New chains of thought and — rah! Feeling nauseous is a good time to stop writing because the product is usually greatly sub-par or, as my kind boyfriend likes to say, 'It's obvious you are on something.'

I am going into school for morning tea, to celebrate my lovely Hobbits' valiant and determined swotting for mocks this past week (and, according to what we tell our parents, months before that too …) I am excited about seeing them all.

My year group is tiny — less than sixty-five girls — and we all share this amazing common room called Hobby. It's the coolest common room ever, actually a house! We all pretty much live there. It means that everyone knows everyone and everything about everyone …which is occasionally a pain. In the long run, though, these girls have been my classmates for seven years and I am sooo lucky to have them.

They are all completely insane in their own glorious way and I HAVEN'T SEEN THEM IN OVER A WEEK. This feels odd because they are my constant, my stability. As you can see from this massive rant, I am very excited to be going to see the girls today, even if I will have to just lie on the couch and be smothered/smother others with hugs.

On this note, I must get ready.

WHAT USED TO TAKE ME FIVE MINUTES
NOW TAKES ABOUT AN HOUR!

DEFINITELY BACK TO BABY STATUS.

THURSDAY, 22 SEPTEMBER 2011

THE HOBBITS

I AM PURELY BLOWN AWAY. I don't know what to think! Is this not one of the most beautiful quilts you have ever seen? I was almost in tears when the girls presented it to me! Every girl in my year created an amazing patch, and they have all been sewn together. It sounds weird, but this is so perfect.

Next year, we all go out into the real world, and many of my closest friends are going to the *opposite* side of the world on their adventures. But I am going to be here, and that sucks.

I was meant to be going with them. I was meant to be, but I am not, and that's hard. The quilt is almost perfect because now I can keep some of each of my friends with me, even when they can't physically

be there. I know that they are with me forever, on this and the other journeys of my life. Sorry about the cheese, but it's true. I love you guys soooooooo much!! I may have needed to grab a few tissues writing this, but — ahhhhh — sooo amazing!!

So much love. I am so lucky to be a Hobbit.

It was nice seeing everyone, too, even though I was really weak and couldn't stand up for very long. I managed to sit out on the lawn in one of the chairs. It made me so happy. One thing that surprised me was the way people were unsure on the topic of whether to visit me or not. COME VISIT ME!!!!!!!!

Seriously, anyone, anytime. Flick me or my parents a text, and *come*. Your company is loved and adored. You don't have to stay for long, or you can stay as long as you want. If I am too sick, I will say!

Bring stuff! Do not feel you need to bring stuff! Just bring you! If you really want to bring something, homebaking is always a hit (my mother, as much as I love her, is no baker). In all seriousness, just bring yourself.

I hope that clears up the debate in your mind of whether to come or not :) and took your mind off my mushiness about how amazing the Hobbits are.

SATURDAY, 24 SEPTEMBER 2011

EVERY DAY IS A GIFT

THE MOULTING IS SLOWLY STARTING. It's the beginning of the bald phase of my life. Oddly enough, the hair is not falling out in huge chunks, instead each individual strand is starting to come loose. I don't even feel it. I thought huge clumps would come out every time I ran my hand through my hair, but they're not. It's just one or two individual hairs at a time.

I thought I would be upset watching my hair go. It sounds stupid, but as an 18-year-old girl, my hair is important to me. I am also strangely excited. I love my wig. It's nicer than my actual hair.

My hair over the years has been so abused by me. In the past three years it has been blonde to chocolate-brown and back again. I have bleached, stripped and coloured my hair about once every two months, and consequently destroyed my mum's wallet and my hair.

Thinking about it, though, hair is such a pain. You have to wash it, brush it, maintain it. It takes soooo much effort and I am so lazy. The idea of whipping on a wig and going out is actually rather appealing. I hope my head is not deformed or something. That could be awkward.

Now onto more important things: THAT TRY LAST NIGHT. I am so unimpressed with the French. If you didn't watch it (you should have) the ref was talking to the All Blacks, and then the French decided to start playing and score a try … and the ref gave it to them! Lucky the French are useless and lost anyway — but *so* not cool.

I was talking to my mate who was watching it with me, and he was right, it may have been a 'legal' try but it wasn't very ethical. The French showed bad sportsmanship with that one. They were losing, and could have lost graciously, but that was a bit of a low blow. It may have been legal, but it left a bad feeling in the stomach.

It's interesting when something like cancer happens because it puts things into perspective. Stupid girly fights = pointless. That perfect dress = might be important still / not really, but hey! — it's pretty! The things that are truly important are people, and doing what you love. Enjoying life. Not putting it on hold. Not doing physics at uni because it will give you a good job, but doing archaeology, which you love. It makes choices simpler. It emphasises living now because who knows what tomorrow will bring.

It also emphasises not dwelling on what could have been, but enjoying what is. Last night I could have had a fat cry about how unfair it was that I wasn't able to go to the Wellington College ball, which I had been looking forward to for months, but instead I had a great night eating fried rice and watching the rugby with a great mate.

ENJOY LIFE, YOU NEVER KNOW
WHAT WILL HAPPEN.

THURSDAY, 29 SEPTEMBER 2011

MY FRIENDS ARE SO LEGIT

My friends. wow. oh. wow.

They are actually so amazing! I do not understand what I did to deserve these children! My friends Harriet and Kat have decided to go insane and shave their hair to match me. This is a really kind gesture. On top of this, they decided to raise money for the Malaghan Institute of Medical Research. If you want to donate, they have set up online donations at:

FUNDRAISEONLINE.CO.NZ/HARRIETROWLAND/

The reason I bother to mention this is because I think cancer research is important — so many people are affected by it — and because I cut my hair on Tuesday.

My hair is slowly falling out, and I decided it was rather annoying having long hair, so I went and got it cut!

The thing that is interesting is the way people look at me now.

I didn't end up being able to go to the Scots' ball which sucked. I made my boyfriend a complete loner. Poor child was MC of the ball and had to turn up dateless. How he puts up with me, I truly have no idea. I decided that there was no way I could make my parents buy me a stunning Juliet Hogan dress and not wear it anywhere, so I dressed up, and hence the photo! Then I made Pan dress up in a suit, and off we trotted to a restaurant called Ancestral.

It was soooo yummy. The food is delicious and I had great company, but I noticed other people in the restaurant looking at us a little oddly, almost questioning why two teenagers were dressed up so nicely and at a restaurant. However, I had a lovely night and it didn't really matter in the grand scheme of things. It's interesting, though, because my new haircut — while being very practical — is unusual for a girl my age interested in guys. As my brother says, it screams 'lesbian', which I think is stupid.

People judge so much about a person from their looks. I guess that's why a uniform is so good. I wonder if judgement based on appearance will ever be redundant, but I don't think so. It is odd, though, because it's something we have very little control over.

The way we appear says a lot about us. There is a reason why goths, for example, dress in a particular way. We all feel we can convey meaning through our appearance, but then get pissed off when people assume things inappropriately or incorrectly.

LIFE IS SOOO ODD.

Today I went up to Auckland and met with my surgeon and discussed my operation. I am going to have a bone graft on my knee, and the surgeon is going to try and save my knee articular surface. In normal language, that's the area where the femur and tibia meet. This is going to be amazing, because it means that if it works I will not have to have a knee replacement at a later date. However, it is going to suck. BIG TIME. This is because when then the tumour is taken out, they will have to replace the bone with dead-guy bone.

Now dead-guy bone is great but it won't attach itself to my bone while I am on chemo. This means that my leg will not be able to have any weight on it for about nine months (if not longer) after surgery. How lame is that?

After this news, I did some great retail therapy and got a lovely maxi dress to hide the brace I have to wear.

Apparently my knee is weak and prone to breaking, and if it breaks there is a high chance they will have to amputate — so, 'Hello, leg brace!' I also bought a groovy orange belt and to-die-for bag. Thank you, Mummy!! I guess there are some upsides to cancer.

SATURDAY, 1 OCTOBER 2011

MIGRAINES ARE NASTY, WITH A CAPITAL N

So unimpressed with this migraine. It ruined my weekend plans. I have been upchucking here, there and everywhere. Thank the gods that I have a legit stockpile of anti-nauseas, because that means it will not ruin my Sunday.

I had a really cool day on Friday, though. It was my school's house music day. The year 13 dance was especially hilarious! Check it out: 'yr 13 item' on Youtube. The video quality is not very good but it does give you a great indication about how awesome the girls in my year are. I actually adore them! The hilarious moments never cease :)

Even more importantly, STIRLING WON!!! (First equal, but shush!!) WE WON!!! We are the house that is known for losing everything. I have always kinda loved it because we were the underdogs … but *this year*, we won!! I must say the house leaders put so much effort into the day, and as always it was amazing.

I cannot mention house music without mentioning the teachers' video. Every year the media teacher makes this hilarious staff video where she gets all the teachers dancing. Every year it's a little bit different, but this year she excelled herself.

I seriously have been so lucky going to Queen Margaret's. It has been a really amazing place to go to school, and I would seriously recommend it. I have enjoyed my time so much. I know I talk about school a lot, but hey! — what can you expect? I am a teenager. School = Life!

Tomorrow I am going to be better. No choice.

BAM!
AND THE MIGRAINE IS GONE …
I HOPE.

MONDAY, 3 OCTOBER 2011

PLAN B

I AM ALMOST COMPLETELY BALD. The beautiful short haircut gone. The past two days I have had to wear my wig or a hat. They are great for feeling normal, but annoying. I want to take my wig off and for there to be hair there. I want this to have been a dream.

It's not a dream, though, it's life. My life. Tomorrow I will be admitted to hospital for three weeks. When that's done I will have two weeks out. In one of which I won't feel very well. I have one week in every five weeks when I am me. I have only fourteen days left of this year when I will feel good.

That sucks because my poor friends will come and visit me, and I will be so happy to see them, but I will be sick. The thing that's so hard is that I cannot see the end. I am only just beginning, but so are all my friends. We are setting out into the world to figure out what we want to be and then finding our 'Plan B'. This is my Plan B and it sucks, but I need to smile or I will start to cry.

Last year this amazing woman called Mai Chen came to our school and talked about how life is nothing but

Plan B. The idea behind her talk was that life never works out how you want it to — it changes in crazy ways, and you need to adapt and work with Plan B.

My plan was to go to Otago Uni. I was going to apply to hostels, and pray to get into one. I was going to do a Bachelor of Science with a major in Psychology and Genetics, and a minor in Bioethics. This was the plan because the courses sounded interesting, and I am interested in them. I was not sure.

Plan B hit me slam in the face. I have cancer. I have to fight it with every fibre of my being. I occasionally get angry because it was not something I wanted. But it's happening, and I cannot turn my back on it. I do not want to go into hospital for three weeks but I will. I'll get through that, then I am going to reward myself. Last night I had lots of friends over to watch the Warriors' game.

WE LOST, BUT YOU KNOW WHAT? THAT DIDN'T MATTER
ONE BIT TO ME BECAUSE I WAS SURROUNDED
BY FRIENDS AND PEOPLE I LOVE. THEY WERE HAPPY
AND, MOST IMPORTANTLY, I GOT PIZZA.

Plan B was not something that I chose but I am going to make the best of it because I only have one life and, seriously, what is the point in being unhappy? Why waste time with it? Life comes quickly, it can go even faster. My life is Plan B. Go figure.

WEDNESDAY, 5 OCTOBER 2011

WARM FUZZIES

HOSPITAL IS NOT GREAT, but I'm feeling much better than I did last time. I am able to hold conversations with many of my visitors, and Ashna, who goes to my school, has written a beautiful song:

SOUNDCLOUD.COM/ASHNA-BASU/YOU-CAN-TAKE-MINE

It made me cry — it is such a beautiful song!!! I adore it. I am a music geek, so this means it is so *much* beautiful!!! Beautiful, beautiful, beautiful. There is nothing else I can say right now!

In other news: Jossi Wells. Jossi Wells is the number one world free-skier and a genuinely lovely guy (check out **jossiwells.com**). When I was down south, I skied

L-R: Sarah, Jossi, Jess and me!

with him, and when I say *skied* with him, I stood in awe!! But hey! — photographic evidence provided.

Jossi sent me an email, which is amazing because being winter, he has so much on his mind. It's insane how many people care, and it matters because this chemo is not fun.

CHEMO MAKES YOU INSANE!

CHEMO BRAIN:

1. I DON'T KNOW WHEN THINGS HAPPEN.
1. I DON'T KNOW WHAT I SAY.
1. I LOSE TRACK OF TIME.
1. I DON'T MAKE A HELL OF A LOT OF SENSE MOST OF THE TIME.

FRIDAY, 7 OCTOBER 2011

WHAT HAPPENS WHEN I DON'T GET MY CHEESEBURGER

IT'S GOOD TO BE FEELING BETTER IN HOSPITAL. The only thing is they need to wake you up all the time to do lots of different checks, but hey! — this means you get a relatively lucid blog update.

The reason I am sure I am feeling better is … if I was listing my emotions right now 'hungry' would be right on top. Luckily I have some chips to satisfy this.

I also know this, because one of the funniest things to happen to me in a while actually happened *in hospital.* I was lying here. In this bed. Which is a single room (jackpot! — no room-mate to complain about this time.) All of a sudden I started to get this real hankering for … a Maccas cheeseburger. So I did the normal thing of texting the boyfriend who was coming in for a visit. He turned up all smiles. With no cheeseburger.

I did not find this acceptable.

His excuse was that he was on the bus.

Somehow in my drug haze, I managed to get my jelly in his hair. I found this so funny, I decided that was exactly where the rest of the jelly should go too. Pan really is a marvel to put up with me sometimes.

It may seem like such a childish thing to do AND it was, but I am child. I am 18. A supposed adult, but not really. I still need my mum to shower me on occasion. I need my family around me to feel safe.

I am an adult with training wheels. Learning and trying to become one, but not quite there … yet.

MONDAY, 10 OCTOBER 2011

INSANITY

I AM OFFICIALLY AN EXCESSIVE OVEREATER. I need to join Overeaters Anonymous. I escaped this place they call the hospital for all of three days, and it was glorious!

I love being at home, and nothing was nicer than sitting outside (yes, it was sunny in Wellington) and chatting with friends — but I'd developed cooped-chicken syndrome. I realised that for ONE WHOLE WEEK I had only been at home or hospital. Nowhere else.

I wanted to get *out.* I was going insane. I was DFHAGFHDGOHAGHUUGFKG!! I am far too social for my own good. I have never spent this much time at home … ever. I have always enjoyed being out and about, and was known for disappearing for entire weekends at a time with my parents relying on intermittent texts for updates on my whereabouts. I must have worried them.

I worry my parents still. I think I always shall. There won't be a time ever that I won't.

I WAS A BIT OF A WILD-CHILD
LAST YEAR, AND THIS YEAR, CANCER …
WHAT NEXT? I AM UNSURE HOW
I AM GOING TO TOP THIS ONE.

I have made my parents live out every parents' nightmare! Oh well, another week of chemo starting today. This week, hopefully, I should be okay. I'll have an amazing chemo brain so beware of my blog. It may become even more riddled with insanity!

MONDAY, 17 OCTOBER 2011

RUGBY? OHHH YEAHHH

Hospitals are odd places. They are a world of their own. They seem to function on their own time and never seem to sleep. There is always something happening.

Today is surgery day! I have to get *another* Hickman line put in! It all started last Friday … I think Mum must have been feeling a bit bad for going away (she was leaving me and going to her university reunion for the weekend). I figured this out when she turned up with not only my favourite sushi but one of the rolls that I love from my favourite bakery, *and* a cream donut! However, I was most impressed, and I think she should go away more if I get food like that.

Anyway she ended up going away and having a marvellous weekend. It was odd, though, because as I was sitting there (nursing my belly after so much good food), I noticed that my shirt on one side was rather wet. I called in my nurse to have a look, and she took one look and promptly informed me that my line was almost out.

The line was supposed to last me the entire time I was on chemo — go figure! I am an odd case.

I went home on Saturday, anyway, much to my pleasure, and I managed to watch the RUGBY!!! OHHHHH YEEEEEAAAAAHHHH!!!!! I really do feel like doing a dance just thinking about the game.

The Welsh should have won, that is the only shame. The French were almost beaten by a fourteen-man side who far outplayed them, but I guess that's life!

I was supposed to start chemo today, but the liver is a little grumpy with me. The liver is affected by methotrexate (one of the types of chemo I get) and it needs to recover to be able to take the next type of chemo. This means the next round has been delayed until my liver function comes to play.

THIS IS LAME BUT THIS IS LIFE!

THURSDAY, 20 OCTOBER 2011

FEARS OF LIFE

I NOW HAVE A BRAND NEW HICKMAN LINE. It was bit of a mission as they had to make two cuts to find a vein big enough. The cut where they found the vein is at the base of my neck just above my collarbone, so it's a bit harder to hide than the one before, but that's okay.

I was more concerned because I was 'nil by mouth' for about twenty-four hours before the surgery. I was sooo hungry!! All I could talk or think about, and just generally BREATHE, was food! I have since caught up on the food I missed.

I am a bit nervous about tomorrow. I have not been that nervous about any of the other rounds of chemo, but tomorrow I am going to start the chemo that makes me incredibly sick. YAY!! Hopefully it should be better than last time because they have my nausea medicine under control, but it's still scary. Lucky me, I have pretty pills which will help. What about everyone else?

What scares me more than the idea of being sick is the idea of being left behind. Nothing scares me more. I know it's crazy, but until August next year I can pretty much give you a schedule of my life. It is basically a five-week cycle where I am living the same five weeks over and over and over and over and over again, but my friends aren't. My friends are facing other huge scary challenges, like leaving school and deciding what to do! — and God forgive them if they *don't* know.

THERE IS SO MUCH PRESSURE
ON PEOPLE MY AGE
TO KNOW WHAT THEY WANT TO DO WITH
THE REST OF THEIR LIVES
BUT WHO REALLY KNOWS AT 18?

Isn't the idea to change and then change some more? But anyway, while my friends are on this adventure of self-discovery, I shall be sitting in the same place.

And this is what scares me most.

In their new lives, how much time will my friends have for me? It's a selfish thought, and it's awful that I am not being more supportive, but hey! — I am nothing if not honest. That is my biggest fear. And birds! Whoever invented those cretinous creatures …

THURSDAY, 27 OCTOBER 2011

NATURE AND THINGS

TODAY IS THE DAY! Today is the day my friends, brother and boyfriend decided to lose their luscious locks in support of me and to raise money for cancer research. Man! How lucky am I? Seriously, not only are *they* doing this but friends are coming from all over Wellington to support them. I seriously cannot believe how lucky I got with my friends.

The thing is, they are my life now. I have no life really, it's rather boring. It's just chemo, sickness, then better — for a small amount of time — then it starts all over, and I have to do this for eight months. So I live vicariously through my friends.

At the moment, because of exams, there is very little scandal, but soon it shall be SUMMER! Not that it looks like it outside ... oh well. Weather is yet another thing we cannot plan. Most people spend their whole lives making plans (I am a very good example of one!) — but what happens when these plans don't work?

I really like biology (nerd right!) and in nature when the environment of an organism changes it will either adapt or die out. It's interesting watching my family (yes, this is as creepy as it sounds) change and adapt to living with cancer.

My mother is a marvellous woman but she has never really been the sort of mum to wait on her children hand and foot. She was always keen for me to try things myself and establish my independence. Yet, I have regressed back to being a baby and need so much help all the time. It's not easy on her.

She is used to constantly doing things and is very bad at sitting still but she, like rest of my family, is slowly adapting … slowly getting used to this new life that I have made them have. Sometimes nature is cruel.

MONDAY, 31 OCTOBER 2011

YAY FOR SICKNESS!!

So I AM NEUTROPENIC. In regular human-speak this means I have no immune system — lucky me! I have picked up some sort of a bug, so it's hospital time.

Onto more exciting things, though. The weekend was amazing. The girls and boys looked seriously attractive with their shaved heads :) In the end, we had five guys and two lovely ladies lopping off their locks!! Thanks to Ben White for the photos. I have stolen them!! They are rather amazing, my dear.

After all the hair had departed heads, we decided to go inside for some good old food, and ate ourselves silly. So, overall, I would say that I had an amazing night, and I hope everyone else did too.

On Saturday I went to my friend Willy's umu. It was so lovely as I got to have a good catch up with lots of mates I hadn't talked to in a while, and ate SUCH YUMMY FOOD. I am going to come out of this like ten tonnes heavier, because all I do is eat, sleep and socialise, which usually involves food.

On Sunday — just to continue the trend of eating — I went to lunch with one of my best mates, Claudia. She is actually one of the most awesome people you could ever know. It also happened to be her birthday. Sadly, my silly bleeding noses put a little damper on the mood.

At some point in my life, I must thank my baby brother, Tom. He drives me everywhere and is just a general cool cat. He brought me chocolate on Saturday (and got into some serious good books with that one!!)

So I went home, driven à la brother, and tried to relax. Dad came home proud as a peacock because he had won the semi-final of his golf tournament and was into the final. I wasn't feeling great, though, so I asked Dad to get the thermometer and BAM! — temperature. So off to ED he took me.

I had one of the creepiest experiences in the ED waiting room. I have a little card to make sure I get whisked through and don't have to wait in the waiting room with millions of sick people, but I sat down to fill out a form and — as I was writing away — along comes the Lady in the Hat.

The Lady in the Hat has very bad eye makeup: panda eyes to rival even Caitlin's sister. She comes over to me and asks, 'Have you seen a car?' I am unsure what to say, so I sit there quietly hoping she will go away. She continues, 'I am new to Wellington and I have lost my car. It's silver.' And she recites some sort of number plate.

She then states loudly that it's HERS, nobody else's, and proceeds to try to give me a cell phone number, so I can text her if I see it. I reply that I have cancer so I spend most of my time in hospital and am unlikely to see her car. She tries to give it to me anyway, and says she could visit me.

Some things are worse than cancer, and I think psychiatric problems are seriously one of the worst things that can happen to a person. Dad came to my rescue, and took me away from the waiting room.

I then had to lie in a bed in a room that smelled faintly of pee for many hours. Father was great and stayed for the whole time, keeping me company. Unlike Mother he can actually sit still, and is very patient. Telling Mother not to come was the wisest thing I ever did.

So that brings us to now, and I am just chilling back in my favourite ward. I have a single room, so no bed-pooping room-mate. I have to get a blood transfusion because my red blood cells are low, as well as antibiotics and a few jabs into my belly. But aside from that … not too much.

My baby brother, Tom,
the skux that he is …

Pan. I now have a skinhead for a boyfriend. How joyous is that?

Don't they look pretty???

Mr James Kane (sorry about the eyebrow).

WEDNESDAY, 2 NOVEMBER 2011

HAPPINESS

As I WAS ROAMING THE INTERNET TONIGHT trying to coax sleep closer. I found this amazing quote and, as most quotes with pretty pictures do, it got me thinking. I like it. I really do.

'THE HAPPIEST PEOPLE
DON'T HAVE THE BEST
OF EVERYTHING,
THEY JUST MAKE
THE BEST OF EVERYTHING.'

It's so simple and yet so true, and it's kinda easy to forget. Everyone is surrounded by crap, and sometimes it's piled so high it's hard to see over.

I will not be the first person to say chemo is crap. I would hate it, but that would involve physically having enough strength to hate it. As I don't have much energy, there's no chance I am wasting my hate on chemo. But it does suck.

There are so many things that cancer has stolen from me — but you know what? Forget it! I am happy.

TODAY I MADE IT OUT OF HOSPITAL.
I HAD STRAWBERRIES MY GRANDMA
BROUGHT DOWN FROM HAWKES BAY, I BOUGHT
THE NEW FLORENCE & THE MACHINE CD,
AND I EVEN ATE A CRUNCHIE!

That's my day today. It may be little things, but hey! — little is better than nothing. That's how I look at life. It's how I have to look at life, because if I counted up the things that I couldn't do because of cancer, I'd literally not be able to stop crying.

FRIDAY, 11 NOVEMBER 2011

THE FIGHT

ONE DAY THIS WILL ALL BE OVER but until then … I just keep on fighting it. It's hard. I will never be able to say it isn't. This week is a testament to that. It was supposed to be my easy week and just … no. It was not, at all. I wish I could fast forward next year, but hey! — life isn't like that.

You get your ups, you get your downs. I've had it pretty easy. I can't believe the things I used to complain about. They seem so silly. So pathetic. Even now there are many people who have it much harder than me.

I tried to make a wish today as it was 11:11 on the 11/11/11. I ended up just being thankful for all the things that I have in my life. I can't tell you my wish but it wasn't for me. It never will be. Don't get me wrong, I wish more than anything that I was a normal teenager. I wish I'd never had to go through any of this. I wish I didn't have to grow up so fast. I wish I could have the wild summer that I'd planned.

But I still have my family and my friends, and I am going to come through this fine. There are those who sit on the sidelines, like my brother, who see how much it hurts me and can do nothing but be there — and who would give anything to be in my place but can't.

Imagine if I don't make it. I don't even like to think about what it would do to my family. I can only begin to imagine the pain families feel who lose their kids or sisters or parents to this thing.

So this is my fight. I will fight as hard as I possibly can because I never want to hurt you.

MONDAY, 21 NOVEMBER 2011

THE NORM

MY MOTHER CONSTANTLY TELLS ME I should update this blog, and I should. Sorry for being rather useless. The thing is, when I go to write on my blog I normally have some sort of reason for updating it — something new has happened or something has changed.

At first it was really easy to update because everything was so new and so different from what I was used to, but living like this — three weeks in hospital, 'two weeks out'— has become my norm. I say 'two weeks out', because every time I have ended up going back into hospital for at least one of them.

What is *not* normal is I got to meet Piri Weepu and Cory Jane. They came to visit me :D (if you don't know who they are, you should). This was VERY exciting. I wish I had actually been more 'with it', though, because I can't remember many of the specifics of what we actually talked about …

I have now finished all of my pre-operation chemo! This is a very YAY! moment, because in my treatment I have three steps:

1. PRE-OP CHEMO
2. THE OPERATION ... DUN DUN DUN
3. POST-OP CHEMO

So once I have the surgery, it's like I am halfway there, even though I still have six to nine months more chemo.

Jannie is over from Germany. Jannie is like my surrogate aunt — she is one of Mum's best friends and has sort of been there all my life. It's been amazing spending time with her! She leaves tomorrow, which sucks, but I can't really complain.

It's hard for me to lie here and think about what I have been doing, because it is so normal now for me. It's kind of amazing what can become normal. I feel normal, yet I still can't stand for more than three minutes without feeling like I just ran a marathon. Who is normal though??

SUNDAY, 27 NOVEMBER 2011

THE RIDICULOUSLY HAPPY

As the title points out, I am ridiculously happy!! I have now been out of hospital for eight days!! This is the longest time I have been out of hospital since I started chemo!!! I have had the most amazing week seeing my friends and feeling normal.

I never thought that little things could give me such pleasure. I am not a religious person, but I feel like I should thank someone because I am so happy. I look at my bed (where the quilt is that the Hobbits made me) and I smile. Life is odd like that, it hands you something downright awful and all you can do is smile at the good.

Today I had breakfast with my brother and my friend Toby. This might sound a little odd but — as I've said before — my brother is a really cool cat. I have been friends with him ever since I was little, and now I'm sick he drives me around everywhere. After breakfast, we tried to do some Christmas shopping, and then I went to a movie with the lovely Pam (who was my nanny for many years), my mother and my grandmother. It was an interesting movie about this choreographer called Pina and her dance troupe.

Later I went to my boyfriend Pan's house and watched him get dressed up in his beautiful Scots' prefect uniform. It left me howling on the floor. I suggest if anyone is feeling down they should watch their boyfriend dress up in a kilt.

I went to dinner with some good friends, which is always a lovely experience. As you can see, life out of hospital is not a bad one. I am seriously and utterly ridiculously happy.

Life is good. I wish everyone shared this thought.

MONDAY, 5 DECEMBER 2011

FROM THE RIDICULOUSLY HAPPY TO THE RIDICULOUSLY NERVOUS

I AM LYING IN A HOSPITAL BED looking out across Auckland. I am in a room with four elderly ladies. Two of them are rather sick and have been sleeping all day, but there is one old lady who is lovely. I have the most beautiful view of the Sky Tower and the city as I happen to be on Floor 14, Ward 75. Even so, I can't help but wish the sky would come and rescue me.

I am so nervous about the surgery tomorrow, I want to cry, scream and put my foot down. I do not want to do it. I want to be a child again. I want to be able to walk. Next year I am not going to be able to walk.

My life is going to get harder. The chemo is going to intensify after the surgery, I am going to be in hospital more, and for a year I am not going to be able to put any weight on my leg AT ALL. My life is already hard. Excuse my French but this is not f**king fair.

The worst thing is I know that I have to do this. It's either this or I will die. That sounds overly dramatic but it's the truth. Those are my options and I have no intention of letting myself die. I can't do that, not to my family or my friends, and most importantly I have a Euro trip, which I planned to take on my parents' credit card.

Next year is going to suck but I am lucky I have the most amazing friends. Life could be so much worse. I could be a hermit and have no friends. My friends have literally not let me be lonely.

I have been out of hospital for the past two weeks (the first time since I started chemo that it has been a full two weeks), and for that time I have been out for nearly every lunch and dinner, and to so many parties.

I have spent so much time with friends that I will treasure. They make me feel normal and give me strength to face tomorrow. Life would be easier if I didn't wake up tomorrow, BUT there are so many good things in life I just have to be strong and get through the bad. The bad may be ridiculously hard, but when I think back over the last two weeks or the past year, I have had so many good times that vastly outweigh the bad.

As the saying goes, 'I am richer in one moment with my friends than if I had all the money in the world.' I am lucky because I have so many moments. Thank you. You — my friends — make me stronger than I ever thought I could be.

MONDAY, 12 DECEMBER 2011

TOMORROW IS ALWAYS BETTER

THE MORNING OF THE SURGERY (6 DECEMBER) I awoke with my family and surgeons around me. The family was giving words of encouragement. The surgeons were trying to make sure I understood the procedure. Inside me there was a war raging: nausea and wanting to curl up like a baby and refuse to go against wanting the surgery to go ahead. As I am 18, I thought this battle was ridiculous — so I just smiled and nodded at everyone.

Luckily for me, I didn't have to face it for long. I was soon surrounded by bewildering blue creatures who probed me with needles (even one in my spine) … and then BAM! All went black. Nine hours later …

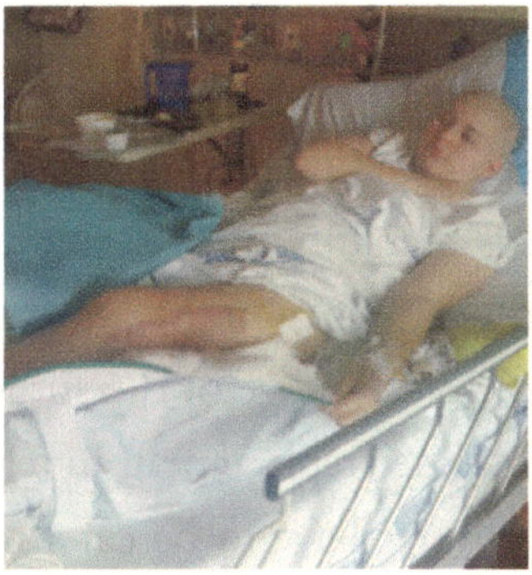

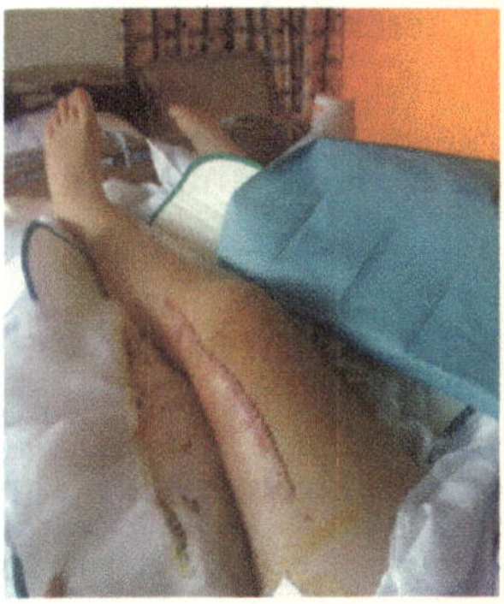

Please note, before I start my explanation, all surgeries have the same end goal: to remove the tumour.

The tumour was located in the bottom of my left femur and, when they were operating, the surgeons realised that it was a large one. This caused problems when it was removed. The surgeons knew if they saved the joint surface, the minute I put weight on it the joint would break. So that was a bummer. Then they tried to do a bone graft with the knee joint from another person, but the bone graft did not fit with my leg properly. I now have a knee that is a mixture of metal, donor bone and my *au naturel* bone. It's a bit of a tight fit to have all three in there, so let's hope the party doesn't get too raucous!

My new knee is awesome, because I might be able to put weight on my leg by January rather than next November!!! This is an amazing advantage as it means that I can go and visit my friends around the world, wherever they are.

With any replacement there are disadvantages. One disadvantage of this surgery is that it is a *partial* knee replacement, so there is metal in my knee. I am going to look like a fool with my pants on the ground in airport security! Another disadvantage of the surgery is that I will need another knee replacement in ten to twenty years, and I will always have to be careful.

After the second knee replacement I will have to have another one, and once that knee replacement has worn out, I may have to get my leg amputated.

I also have to live a careful life. This means no skiing, no running … and I will have to be careful of my weight. That perhaps is not such a bad thing — but I love food sooo much!!

PLUS I HEAR THE SCARS ARE PRETTY IMPRESSIVE, AND HELP US GET THEM BOYS. WHO NEEDS MILKSHAKES?

Over the past couple of days I have been in a lot of pain as we have had some problems with the pain medication, but finally we've sorted most of it out. I have been really lucky, though, because my whole family and Pan (my boyfriend) and Ollie (one of my seriously amazing friends) and Sophie and Alice (my cousins), and lots of other friends and family, have visited me here in Auckland hospital.

I went through a dark patch while my pain medication wasn't working. I felt this huge weight on my shoulders and could see no way of ever getting past it, but Pan and Ollie were there reminding me I wasn't alone. I would then think about the Hobbits, which made things easier. I was going through a hazy sort of consciousness, and Pan and Ollie and my friends stuck with me through it reminding me that things would get better because they always do.

TODAY
WITH THE PHYSIO
I WALKED
ONE METRE
ON A
GRANDMA-WALKER.

I MADE IT.

It is getting better. I never thought it would but it is. Let's see what tomorrow brings.

P.S. Thanks to everyone who sent flowers, chocolates, presents and cards! They are all so lovely and they mean a lot to me.

FRIDAY, 16 DECEMBER 2011

MY BIG OUTING

Today I went on a huge outing! Since my surgery on 6 December I have not left my room. I have barely even left my bed. So today my mother and my lovely nurse, Sarah, got me into a wheelchair, and I managed to get down to Muffin Break!

This is such an achievement!! I was so happy, I mean how many people are cool enough to go to Muffin Break in a hospital gown, fist-pumping in a wheelchair? If only some grandmas had decided to accept my challenge and race me …

I have also been lucky up here, because my friends Nick and Jess have been amazing in coming to visit me heaps. Otherwise I would get rather lonely. I am excited because I should be going back to Wellington on Tuesday. Back to Wellington hospital … and, hopefully, home before Xmas!

I think we deserve a nice drink. Take heed from my mother and her friend Jane:

G&T coz they're classy like that

WEDNESDAY, 21 DECEMBER 2011

HAPPY AND HOME!

I MADE IT! I am back in Wellington! I have set up residence in Bed 1 on 6 North. I am so happy to be home. Auckland Hospital was something very special. It was … useless. Completely and utterly useless. Don't get me wrong — my surgeon is amazing, he did such a fabulous job, but the nurses …

Actually, I had this one wonderful nurse: Sarah. I was very lucky to have her for as long as I did, but most of the other nurses were useless. On the first day after the surgery the epidural did not work properly, which meant I was in so much pain. I had involuntary tears pouring down my face, and I was like this for two, nearly three, hours while the nurses tried to find a doctor.

My mother was unimpressed. She became like a mother lion protecting her cub. I would not have wanted to be on the end of that rampage. It was so different to Wellington. In Auckland we had to ask to see the physios, in Wellington today I have had heaps of help from two physios who spent a lot of time with me. My leg has got better in leaps and bounds. In Wellington, when I call for pain medication they actually bring it, whereas in Auckland I was sometimes waiting up to an hour.

In Auckland, I had to have help getting to the bathroom. The nurse would usually wait outside and then help me back to my bed. However, one lovely nurse decided that while I was on the toilet it would be a great time to go for a break and leave me sitting there. My legs turned blue and got progressively sorer and sorer as blood pooled in them.

It was amazing to see Jess and Nick up there (my friends who live in Auckland). They are some of the nicest people you have ever met. They helped to keep me sane along with Pan and Ollie, who flew up from

Wellington to keep me company. I was very lucky and got a ride home in the medical airplane.

It was such a weird feeling. As you can see in the photo, the beds face the wrong way round. You are looking from the front of the plane down to the back. It was strange taking off that way — pushing forward and leaning oddly on my seatbelt. This led to me having a little freak-out that the bed would come unlocked and roll into the back of the plane. I think I prefer travelling the right way round.

Today in Wellington I have been so lucky and seen so many friends. Seeing everybody makes me happy. I have missed all my friends terribly and I am very happy to be home.

Cross fingers I am out in time for Christmas!

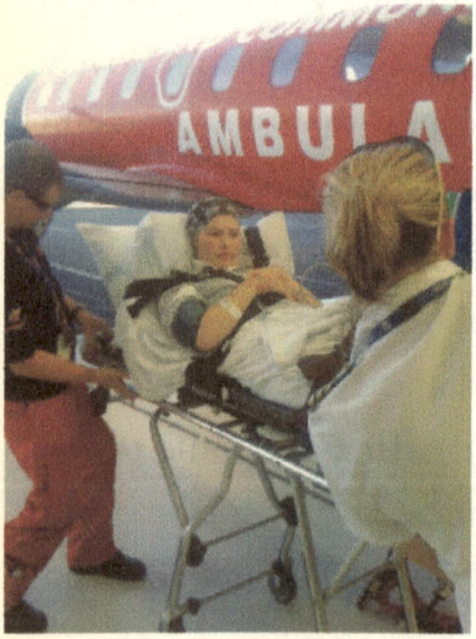

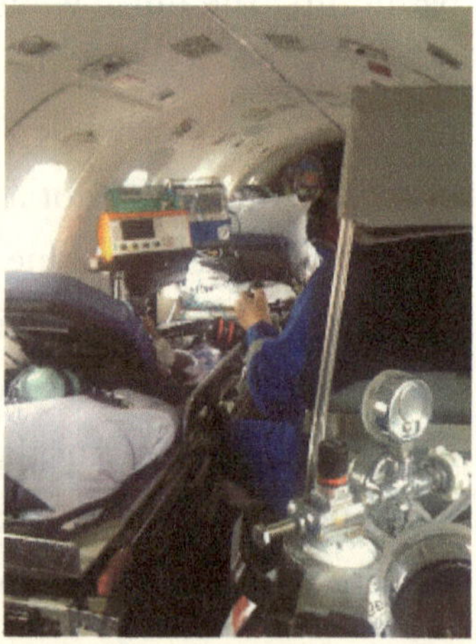

SUNDAY, 25 DECEMBER 2011

MERRY CHRISTMAS

GUESS WHAT …

I GOT TO GO HOME FOR CHRISTMAS !!!!!!!!!!!!!!!!!!!!!!!!

This was actually amazing. The entirety of my mum's side of the family also came out to our house! It was so lovely, as some of them had to come from Aussie. I was spoilt this Christmas!

It was such a wonderful day and I enjoyed it so much. I hope everyone else had as amazing a day as I did.

GREAT FOOD &
AMAZING FAMILY
WHAT MORE
CAN I ASK FOR?

THURSDAY, 29 DECEMBER 2011

NOT SO GOOD NEWS

Today we had some news that left Dad a bit red around the eyes. My histology results. If these were like my history results I'd be okay. You see, histology results are about cell necrosis, and cell necrosis looks at the percentage of cancer cells that are killed by chemotherapy. My oncologist was hoping for a 90% kill rate. Unfortunately, we've only got a 40% kill rate.

This sucks. It means that the next lot of chemotherapy is going to be much harder on me as stronger and even more potent chemicals are added. Joy to the world.

On a happier note, the operation went well from an oncologist's point of view! So I am very happy about that. I am home for another ten days to two weeks before I start the next round of chemo.

N.B. An oncologist is the person who controls my chemo, not a vag doctor.

FRIDAY, 6 JANUARY 2012

HOW ODD IS LIFE

TONIGHT AFTER PAN WENT HOME I WAS FEELING A LITTLE NOSTALGIC for better times. Not because we fought, but because I had to tell him about the not-so-good news. He has been on a walk (not a tramp, he lies if he tells you it was) and hadn't read my latest blog post. It was harder than telling anyone else.

He has already been through so much with me, and never once complained when I told him *yet again* to get me more food, or to get me this or that. He has been amazing, and more than I deserve. He even puts up with me when I am totally spaced-out on drugs and trying to convince him that he should have rampant gay sex with my brother, or when I'm putting jelly in his hair, or any other of the million of things I do. I hated having to tell him that things hadn't gone our way, and they were going to get harder yet.

I was looking through my Photo Booth photos. I have had Photo Booth since year 9, and my friends are the biggest photo whores I know. Thank you Anthony, Rebekah, Rahera, Claudia and the millions of people who made so many hilarious poses and facials.I found a few photos, which reminded me how unpredictable life can be.

LIFE CAN CHANGE IN AN INSTANT SO APPRECIATE EVERYONE.
WHO KNOWS WHAT IS AROUND THE CORNER.

This was taken just over a year ago on the day I decided to go blonde. Again.

This beautiful photo I took with Jess in the July school holidays, one month before my diagnosis.

I got my hair cut short once it started falling out.

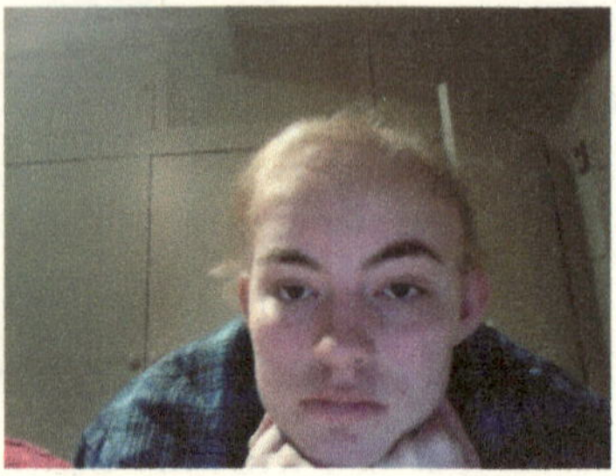

This was taken in my last set of chemo before surgery.

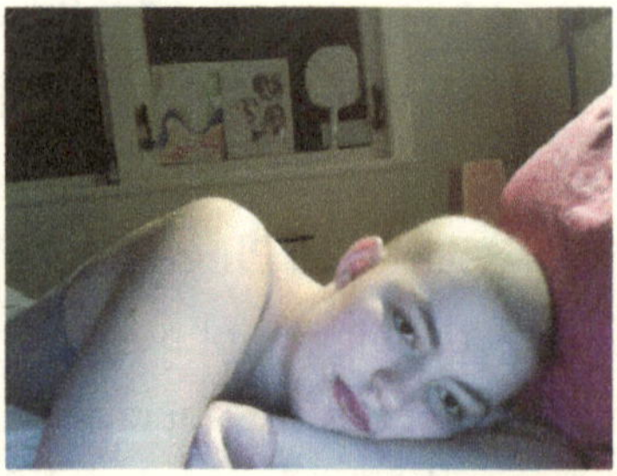

Tonight. HAIR IS GROWING BACK!

MONDAY, 16 JANUARY 2012

LET'S HOLD HANDS AND START AGAIN

TONIGHT, WELL I GUESS IT'S ACTUALLY MORNING, I am sitting here with (a bit) shell-shocked Anthony. He has just seen the X-rays of my leg, and I think I scared him a bit. Which is fair enough, as he can be scared. He's been one of my best friends throughout all of this.

Some girls are a bit mean about him because they think that he is 'flaky' and 'a typical gay guy', but I am here to tell you he is totally *not.* He is amazing. He entertains me even on my worst days and never fails to bring a smile to my face.

I really wish everyone had the pleasure of meeting him. He is one of the best people I have ever known. He worries about studying in Otago, but I am sure he will be fine as — because of all the reasons mentioned above.

I have to start chemo again tomorrow, lame right? I am nervous and a bit worried because my oncologist, Anne, said that it would be harder than most, because my body is not used to it anymore, and it also happens to be the type of chemo that makes me really sick so YAY … not really.

I have only got one week in hospital so that's good and then I will have another two weeks out. Tom and Dad have gone away, though. This sucks. For anyone that doesn't know, my dad and my brother are both my friends. They are awesome, and when I am in hospital they come in every afternoon after school and every night after work and feed me.

I am going to miss them heaps. I am a little worried I am going to get lonely in hospital, because everyone is so busy right now enjoying the sun (very little of it ever hits Wellington). Loneliness sucks because there is nothing I can do about it, and when I am on chemo I am too sick to do a lot of things, so finding a distraction can sometimes be hard.

I am saved when I have visits. People are the most interesting distraction. I love hearing about their lives, because everyone has different experiences and problems.

PEOPLE ARE INTERESTING.

WEDNESDAY, 25 JANUARY 2012

DANCING IN THE RAIN

THIS MORNING I WOKE UP to such a lovely message from one of the girls I went to school with. She'd found a quote on the internet and thought of me. This is so lovely in itself, but it meant more because I have been having a really hard week with chemo. Last week was the worst chemo yet.

I actually chucked my guts up, which has never happened before. Rather impressive when you consider that in hospital I have a pump that injects two different anti-nausea drugs into my arm. I also take a drug called aprepitant, as well as multiple steroids and about five forms of oral tablets to try to keep the nausea at bay. They've worked, until now.

I have also been given a rough end date. If everything goes to plan, I should be done with all of this by early August. Apart from feeling glum, because I have been feeling so sick and I'm missing my brother and dad (they are skiing in the US of A for ten days), I have been kinda irritated. It took me a while to work out why. I figured it was down to the fact that I just want the chemo to be over now. I have really had enough of feeling sick and not having enough energy to walk anywhere or do anything. I just want it to be done *now.* In short, I think I've hit a five-month wall. I still have another seven to go.

The quote my friend sent me was by Vivian Greene:

LIFE IS NOT ABOUT WAITING FOR THE STORMS TO PASS.
IT'S ABOUT LEARNING HOW TO DANCE IN THE RAIN.

This is so true. It made me think about my feelings, and I have now finally come to the conclusion that it is stupid to waste my time being irritated. I can't change the fact that there is still another seven months. Moaning and groaning about how long I have left will only put me in a bad mood. I am in the middle of the biggest hurricane of my life. It's battering me every which way. I can hardly walk, but I am doing everything I can with a smile. In the end the storm will pass.

FOR NOW I AM GOING TO DO MY UTMOST BEST
TO BE THE MOST OBNOXIOUS DANCER IN THE RAIN.

WEDNESDAY, 25 JANUARY 2012

I ADORE YOU, ANNE!!!

ANNE O'DONNELL IS MY ONCOLOGIST. She is a seriously amazing woman — so kind and hard-working — and has given me the BEST NEWS EVER!!!

Anne just called me to say that she sent off my histology results for a second opinion because clinically my leg had improved so much. She is amazing like that — she wanted to be sure. My leg had stopped being sore and everything pointed towards the idea that the chemo HAD WORKED.

And guess what? IT HAD! The second opinion came back different from Anne's. So then she sent it to The World Expert who said that the kill rate of the cancer cells is actually 98%!!!!!!!!!!!!!!!!!!!!!!!!!!!!!!

This means that I now don't have to have the worse chemos!!!!!!!! AND EVEN BETTER … my prognosis for kicking the cancer is, conservatively, at 80%!!!!!!!!!!

ANNE O'DONNELL, I REALLY
DO LOVE YOU.

FRIDAY, 27 JANUARY 2012

THE LIFE OF AN ADDICT

I HAD A BRAIN WAVE THIS MORNING. This does not happen often, but it was so obvious it's crazy. I have finally managed to completely stop taking morphine, which is nice because it means that the pain is getting less and less.

I realised this morning that the reason I have been feeling so sick is because I have been feeling the symptoms of withdrawal. I stopped taking morphine on Sunday, and it was quite odd because I've felt sick and horrible since, with chills and sweats, diarrhoea, insomnia and random shooting pains.

I attributed everything to the fact that chemo had been so horrible, but normally by this point the only residual effect is less energy. It sucks so much that I still have to feel sick, but now I blame it on morphine withdrawal.

I actually ate so much food on Thursday when I got the good news, that I made *myself* sick. Mum was out at a work dinner, so poor Pan and my friend Kate had to clean it up. They are seriously such good friends. I owe them BIG TIME!!!

I am excited because Dad and Tom are coming home tomorrow! I used to complain about my family like every teenager I know: 'Mum won't get me this.' 'Dad said I can't go to that.' But you know what? I am so *lucky* to have had an experience that has opened my eyes so much. I have such an amazing family. Poor Mum has had to run around after me like a house elf because I haven't been able to do much. She is so lovely — she doesn't even complain.

On the topic of lucky, I have officially dated Pan for five months today, which is pretty impressive considering he asked out a girl he knew had cancer. He is the stuff of legend. He is literally so amazing to me. He helps me out with anything and is always there. He even lets his brother and me stick a beautiful temporary tattoo on him — a pink heart made out of flowers. So …

I MAY BE AN ADDICT
BUT AT LEAST
I AM A LUCKY ONE.

TUESDAY, 31 JANUARY 2012

I AM GOING TO LIVE!!!!

I AM SO HAPPY, IT'S HARD TO DESCRIBE HOW I AM FEELING. I keep on randomly breaking into tears because I am soo happy. I can't stop laughing, crying and smiling out of sheer joy.

When I got my bad histology results, I had to come to terms with the fact that I was unlikely to live past the age of 20. At 18 years old, I had to face the fact that it was unlikely that I would live long enough to see my brother start university.

I started to look over my life and appreciate how lucky I had been. I have had one of the most amazing lives. Most people don't get to see the sun set in Africa or the beauty that is the sunflower fields in the south of France; explore Petra (a city that was lost for hundreds of years); sail on the Turkish seas; ski in the mountains of Japan, America and Canada; and so many more experiences.

Then I thought about the people I love and would leave behind. I thought about what I could do to make losing me easier for them. I thought about how I could make the fact that they'd lost a sister, a daughter, a niece, a best friend, not so bad … I thank God for the luck I've had and the life he's let me live. To have so many amazing experiences and to be introduced to so many amazing people …

When I had my bad histology results, I accepted the fact that I would not grow to be old, and that I had to say goodbye to those I loved. I was thinking about not continuing with chemo because I didn't want to spend the little time I had being sick. And now I am going to live, I don't have to think about how my death would hurt those who love me so much. I am so unbelievably grateful for this. So unbelievably happy. I start randomly crying because I am happy that I AM GOING NOWHERE!

I AM GOING TO LIVE !!!!!!!!!!!!!

FRIDAY, 10 FEBRUARY 2012

I COULD NEVER ASK FOR BETTER

I AM SO CLOSE YET SO FAR. My methotrexate levels are 0.02 too high. This is soo annoying as I got them down — from being in the hundreds to 0.08 — but I guess this is what my life is: waiting to be told that I am adequately healthy, and then being dragged back, sick yet again.

The end is in sight but not so close that I can begin to get really excited. On this day in a term and a half I will be dancing like there is no tomorrow, and that's because there will be no chemo tomorrow, or hopefully ever again. But that is about fifteen weeks away.

At the moment I am having to say goodbye to my friends. They are all moving on with their lives. It was very hard last night because one of my best friends, Toby, came in to see me. I am going to have afternoon tea with him on Monday, but this was the last time of just being us. I couldn't really help it — I am rather ashamed, but I was a bit of mess. As with so many of my friends, he has been here week in week out.

Chemo is hard but not just for me. It's hard for everyone. My friends who have watched me going from the overly social, healthy 18-year-old to nothing more than a shell, so sick that I hardly remember what I've said. My friends have been there for it all. I couldn't ask for a better group. So thank you for being there, and I love you.

MONDAY, 13 FEBRUARY 2012

ANOTHER WEEK

IT'S FINALLY HERE. You are all leaving. HELP!!!! I may be a little bit of an emotional wreck this week. I am about to let my Anthony and millions of others onto the world. It's odd because I have known that this point in time is coming for a while … but now it's finally here.

Toby was over. Toby, for all those who don't know, is amazing — one of the coolest cats you will ever meet. Anyway on Monday we were lying on my bed listening to music and chatting, when I realised that I won't have the beautiful pleasure of being in his company for a while …

Today is Valentines Day! Joy for commercialism, but hey! — Pan wrote me a card and in it he wrote, 'My favourite thing is when we just … are. A simple moment. Quiet. Unassuming. And then you say something and suddenly the world seems beautiful … different. Clearer.' This is so true, not only of Pan but of all my friends.

I just love being with you: Toby, Ollie, Caitlin, Jess, Hannah, Kate, Sarah … I could go on forever. I have that many amazing friends. I hope you all know how amazing you are to me. Just spending time with me in hospital … I know it's hard, but thank you.

I do go insane in here. Visits from everyone make me sane. Well, as sane as I ever am. But GOD HELP ME — I AM GOING TO MISS YOU!!!!!!!!

SUNDAY, 19 FEBRUARY 2012

I AM DIFFERENT

I FINALLY DID IT. I changed my Facebook profile picture to one that actually looks like me. I know it seems like something stupid but I love looking at the photos of me with hair. I really was quite pretty but, as much as I hate to admit it, that was a lifetime ago.

Tonight at dinner with my family we were talking about last year. As Tom said, 'I have memories from when I was eight years old that seem more recent than that time.' We have been stuck in here for a long time now.

It was hard last week: there were problems with my Hickman line. This is the third one, and if I have to get it taken out … well … let's just say painful is an understatement. A Hickman line, which has to be put in surgically, is literally tugged out, no anaesthetic needed. More importantly it messes with my schedule. I have started to plan things for the future and things for now. It's hard because a lot of my friends left for uni last week, and I may have got a little lonely in hospital. To make it easier, I am trying to organise things in the time I have to look forward to. I have also invested in some more colouring-in books.

DON'T YOU THINK MY POSTMAN PAT IS BEAUTIFUL?

FRIDAY, 24 FEBRUARY 2012

A CRY FOR HELP

HELP NEEDED. I have been put in a double room. I need as many visitors as possible.

1. I am bored but too sick to do much.
2. The more visitors I have the more likely I am to get complaints (and they might move me!)

The stories of O Week are awesome!! I miss you all like mad but glad to see you're having a good time.

I am in Bed 35, Pod C, Ward 5 North, and should be here til Monday lunch!!

Love you all!

XOXO

FRIDAY, 9 MARCH 2012

A NOT-SO-QUICK UPDATE

I HAVE NOW BEEN IN BED FOR SO LONG I have officially got bed sores! The past three weeks have been rather rotten. I ended up having to have my Hickman line replaced not last Thursday but the Thursday before. The other one ended up having a rip in it. Who knows how that happened.

On the Friday (yes, the very next day!) I started chemo, but one little thing was different from usual. They forgot to give me the aprepitant and steroids, so as soon as the chemo started so did the vomiting. I threw up every pill, and was vomiting for about two hours until the nurses were able to get it under control. That combined with the general anaesthetic (for the Hickman line) and taking Cisplatin meant I was left feeling rather rotten.

I managed to get out of hospital on the Monday, only to have to go back in on Wednesday because of a temperature. Luckily I was not neutropenic this time and was sent home with antibiotics. I was still quite rotten all week. We had our friends come up from Christchurch for the weekend and it was absolutely amazing to see them. I wish I had been better, but I guess that's not how life goes. On Sunday I ended up having to come back into hospital. I was much sicker.

I had developed severe mucositis, which meant I couldn't eat or drink anything because my throat was so raw. This left me miserable. To top it off my immune system decided it had had enough and I was neutropenic again. Also my red blood cell levels were very low so I had to have two blood transfusions, my platelets were low so I had to have two platelet transfusions, and I had low magnesium and potassium. On Monday I got a migraine, which left me throwing up and feeling generally awful.

I am finally feeling better and hopefully will be leaving hospital tomorrow.

LET'S HOPE THE SUN WILL SHINE TOMORROW.

TUESDAY, 13 MARCH 2012

THE CUTEST WEE VISITOR

I HAD THE CUTEST WEE VISITOR YESTERDAY. I left hospital late Saturday afternoon, and spent a lovely Sunday and Monday catching up with a few close friends ... and my adorable new one. Her name is Penny and she is ten weeks old! She is so cute I thought I would share.

FRIDAY, 16 MARCH 2012

WHAT WE DREAM ABOUT

I FOUND A PHOTO while I was doing my nightly hunting on the internet. It's a famous photo of a girl who has had chemo and is drawing hair on her reflection in the mirror because she has none. Sometimes you feel a connection with a photo and this one happened to catch my eye. I wondered why.

I think it's because I seem to spend all of my time in hospital, and all I want to do is go back to the time when life was easy and carefree. It's true I may have partied too much once, but the way I figured it, life was precious and I had no intention of wasting it.

I want to do so much now but I physically can't. I am unable to walk THREE HUNDRED metres without feeling like I've done a marathon. It's so hard because I have been doing this for so long and I just cannot wait for it to be over.

I dream of the days when I can be like everyone else. When my parents yell at me for spending too much money or my brother gets pissed off because I keep on trying to offload my jobs onto him … or when I am not a burden on my family.

They are amazing and never complain, but I know it's soo hard on them because this has taken over their lives. It's not that I don't appreciate their support, because I do, but I just wish that this had never happened to them.

They are very good people.

WEDNESDAY, 21 MARCH 2012

THE BODY DOTH PROTEST

My body has decided to stage a revolt. It has had enough of what I have been putting it through and has decided that enough is enough. I went into hospital on Tuesday morning feeling pretty crap because Pan and I had broken up the night before, and I was just generally under the weather.

As I was sitting in the waiting room my breakfast decided that it didn't like my stomach, so up it came. It turns out that my entire digestive tract has become inflamed and irritated, so the food is going to come out one way or another, and hurt like no tomorrow doing it.

So I have had to put off doing chemo this week as my body is healing itself, which involves me drinking some foul concoction three times a day, having salt baths and doing more random doctorish things that I love so much.

SO YAY
FOR THIS WEEK
AND BEING
NOT SO HEALTHY.

SUNDAY, 8 APRIL 2012

EASTER-FILLED FUN

I AM FINALLY HOME. I have a sore throat, but lucky for me my temperature is not sky-high — for now anyways :) I had an amazing Easter and ate way too much chocolate and left myself feeling rather sick, thank you anti-nausea drugs!!! I hope everyone else was naughty and ate way too much, too. Otherwise I am way too badass for my own good.

I think I kinda rule out being a badass considering I have spent the last two months in hospital. It's hard keeping up your 'badass' pretence when you are as sick as a dog!! But I am finally out, and Anthony is back!!!! As is nearly everyone from uni!!!!

I'm excited because I can see the end of the treatment but … ahhh … first, another three-week block starting next Monday. Until then I am a free chicken! As long as I don't start to roast and get temperatures, if so hospital will be mine again.

My mum went on her 'Girls' Walk' in the middle week of my treatment. It was our first big separation since this treatment started and it was surprisingly hard. She now knows everything about it and is very good at organising me. I think she missed me too because look what she brought back!!! Each time I have had surgery, I have been a little cheeky and teased Mum about how she doesn't want me to have another op because it means she'll owe me another charm on a Tiffany & Co. charm bracelet. I never actually thought she would get me one (Tiffany & Co. is a place that mothers shop not Harriets), but she surprised me with this beauty!! I have five pretty charms, not six, because apparently six looked a bit odd.

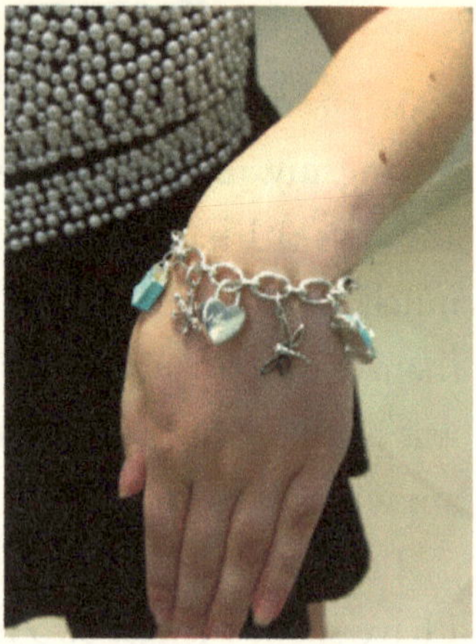

I am wearing it in hospital because I may have been allowed out one night last Saturday night to attend my friend Catherine's wedding!!!! I must give my big congrats.

One week later I went and saw Geraldine Brophy's new play *Floral Notes*. It was very good, apart from Geraldine's character happening to get breast cancer and die. I hate movies and books to do with cancer.

Originally when I got sick I kept everything I was given on the subject, but as time went on I realised it depressed me to read about it.

Ollie probably knows more of the specifics of my treatment. I just take it as it comes and try not to look forward too far. It depresses me sometimes, because although I can see the end of my treatment I still have more to go.

Strangely I think my hair is starting to grow back! Even though I am having chemo I am not taking Cisplatin, so maybe that's the one that makes you lose your hair. I have now a nice sprinkle of stubble on my head!!!!!

Gosh, life is sooo odd. Let's just eat more chocolate!!!

SUNDAY, 15 APRIL 2012

MY PUPPY!!!

My mummy got me a puppy! However, it wasn't really the sort of puppy I was expecting … let me introduce you to Hugo (and a happyish looking Maja). He may not be exactly what I asked for, but as Maja says, 'It's the closest thing to a dog you are getting from me.' So I will just have to love Hugo with all my heart, and accept that a cute wee puppy may not be very attainable.

As for actual progress, I seemed to be healthy the first couple of days out of the hospital, but it went downhill from there. From about Wednesday on everything I ate or drank ended up coming out of me one way or another, neither pleasant.

So it's now Monday and I am back in hospital and will reside here for a good couple of weeks. Things better be getting close to the end, because I am not sure how much more my poor body will take.

MONDAY, 23 APRIL 2012

WOULD YOU FEED THIS TO YOUR DOG?

I HAVE NOT EXACTLY HAD THE BEST COUPLE OF WEEKS. Last I wrote on here, Maja had just brought me Hugo while she was down south with her friends for her birthday. The next day (the day before I was due to be re-admitted anyway), I ended up going back into hospital because I was very unwell.

I couldn't eat much. Anything I tried to eat I would vomit or it would end up coming out in some lovely diarrhoea, so I wasn't getting any nutrients in. I put my parents through hell sometimes. Now I have to quote my dad about what happened because unfortunately I have no recollection of the following events:

> *On Wednesday night just after Tom left, Harriet was found unconscious and unrousable by a nurse checking on her room-mate. They called the crash team, and Harriet came around slowly. She had had a convulsion, not witnessed, so we don't know how long for. She had a CT scan of her head overnight — that was normal — but she has ECG abnormalities, and low potassium and other electrolytes. Harriet was transferred to the coronary care unit for monitoring. She was quite out of it overnight and her brain has not been functioning well since, but at least she doesn't remember anything.*

I can't remember anything much since last Wednesday, in fact. As my friends Sophie and Ollie discovered last night when I had no memory of their visit on Friday.

After the convulsion, my oncologist Anne has decided that it is too dangerous to continue with chemo — so it's all over. I still have to come in at least once a week for a while to do tests and stuff, and apparently next week I could be quite sick because I am coming off all the drugs, which my body has got used to.

It was interesting talking to Mum today about all my medications, especially one called cyclizine. I did not know, but when it is given through the IV line it can be addictive. I hate the idea that I could be addicted to something, but I do wonder if I was — just a little.

I know I like it because it is the drug that works best. I can take three different pills and then half an hour later, hopefully, I will feel better. Or I can have cyclizine, and five minutes later I feel better. It does work very well and that's great, because up until now all I have cared about is not vomiting, and feeling functional and all that. It is scary how easily you can get addicted.

To be fair, if my mum had told me cyclizine could be addictive, I probably would have just stopped taking it because I hate the idea of becoming dependent on something. I still like cyclizine, though, because it works so well — but what if I am wrong about it?

I am very happy because I am going to be finished with chemo. It's going to take me about a month or two to feel normal again but I can handle that. What's two months in the grand scheme of things? It's weird, because it sort of just stopped. I still thought I had another month and a half of chemo to go, and now I am of reeling. I want to say it's an amazing feeling — and it is — but there is that feeling, too, of it being too good to be true.

I'm done, but now what? I actually have no clue. I have spent the past eight months geared towards getting to this point, but now what? I am in limbo because I am not better ... but I am not having chemo anymore.

Anyway I thought I would leave you with some food for thought. I have avoided eating hospital food for the last eight months by getting family and friends to bring me a constant supply of what I need. Why? you ask. A picture can't leave you with a proper impression of the smell, but would you feed your dog this?

SATURDAY, 5 MAY 2012

THE BRAIN DANCE

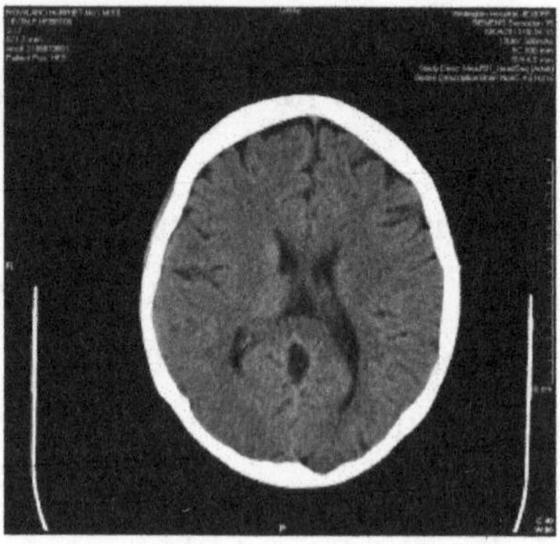

I WOULD LIKE TO INTRODUCE YOU TO SOMETHING that is very dear to me. My darling reader, I would like you to meet my completely normal brain. When I had the seizure, the main concern was for my brain and a brain haemorrhage.

A brain haemorrhage is a type of stroke caused by an artery in the brain bursting, and causing localised bleeding and killing brain cells. Well, this lovely, beautiful and completely wonderful scan shows that my brain is perfectly healthy and normal. So I am doing a little dance for my perfectly healthy brain.

FRIDAY, 11 MAY 2012

THE SILVER SCREEN

THIS NEW HARRIET CERTAINLY GETS COLD EASILY, and I say 'new Harriet' because I think it sounds better than 'post-cancer Harriet'. This is what I will always be now. The people who meet me from now on will probably think of me as 'that chick who had cancer', and I guess I am. It's not like I want to wear it as a badge of honour but I don't really have a choice.

My scars will stay with me for the rest of my life no matter how much bio oil I use. People will ask, 'How did you get that?' because who would expect the reply? The reply I am thinking of giving is, 'I saw this kid getting beaten up, I ran over to help and the guy pulled out a knife. He managed to get me a few times but at least the kid got away.' When I get, 'Really?!?!' I, of course, will confess the truth — but which would you believe?

I am still at home and my immunity is going down again. It kills me a little because it's hard, and because I want to go out and party and dance and be ridiculous … but I can't. My leg is getting better but I still can't really walk properly. I have a limp. At least that's progress.

The local video hire has become my new best friend. My brain has been really fried so I am trying to read, but I am still struggling with magazines, so blobbing and watching endless movies passes the time well. I seem to have a lot of it, and everyone seems to be busy during the week with uni and work.

And so begins my love affair with the silver screen.

SATURDAY, 19 MAY 2012

THE OREO LIFE

I WAS STALKING THE INTERNET AND I FOUND THIS random cartoon that got me thinking. It had a picture of the Mayan calendar and one of an Oreo cookie — they looked almost the same — and it said:

Pessimist's view:
The world will end on December 21, 2012.

Optimist's view:
2012 is the 100th anniversary of the Oreo cookie.

Today was a rather big day!! I went out for lunch with some of my friends and then I went back to my friend's hostel and hung out with her and her new friends, and then I went out to dinner with some other friends!!!!!! I WAS OUT FOR SEVEN HOURS!!!

I cannot remember the last time I managed this, to be fair I was sitting down the whole time, but at least I was able to be out!!! I have been kind of pessimistic the last few weeks as I have been feeling rotten and glad chemo is over, but I have still been grumbling about being sick. As my wise friend said, 'Things are looking up, oh finally!!'

FRIDAY, 25 MAY 2012

MONSTERS UNDER THE BED

I HAVE MONSTERS UNDER MY BED. I have even more monsters in my head. I hate sleeping. It's really awful. I always used to think that sleeping was such a waste of time but now I hate it for a new reason. The dreams won't stop coming. They aren't even dreams. I have nightmares.

They started about a week and a half ago and now I have them every time I close my eyes. I have never really had nightmares before, but they scare me like no tomorrow. Last night I managed to get to sleep at about midnight, and at about 2am I woke up and couldn't handle being in my room. I had to get up and go on the Exercycle to try and clear my head. When that didn't work I ended up watching cartoons for hours trying to get the nightmare out of my head.

I could deal with the nightmares if they were to do with the usual things: spiders or heights, but of course they are about cancer. For example, last night I dreamed I was suddenly in the most excruciating pain (it was like after my surgery when the epidural didn't work). I saw a little morphine tablet on the table next to me. I took it trying to get rid of the awful pain, but it turned out to be full of maggots, which started eating me inside out. Suddenly they became restraints holding me to a vertical bed, and I had to sit and watch as a procession of people had chemo injected into them, and I could do absolutely nothing but watch.

I HATE GOING TO SLEEP
BECAUSE THERE ARE
MONSTERS IN MY HEAD.

WEDNESDAY, 30 MAY 2012

AND OFF I GO!!

I DROVE, AND IT WAS SO MUCH FUN!!! I forgot how much I like to drive. My mother and father got a manual car when my baby 'Bruce' decided to give up on life. I am not ashamed to say that I suck at driving a manual, as I learned how to drive in an auto, and it sapped a lot of my confidence. I am VERY uncoordinated and it just didn't come naturally. About two weeks before my diagnosis I was finally getting it, but my confidence had suffered a lot and I stopped enjoying driving so much.

This is more than just about being able to drive. It means I am no longer stuck in my house. My friend Ollie came over last week after I had spent the day alone and at home, and I may have gone a bit insane. Just a tad. He picked up on this, and compared me to a cooped-up chicken.

There is only so much daytime TV you can watch, and after a while you just need to get out. The best thing about having a car is that I finally have the freedom to do that! It may be a small step but it's a step, and I intend to celebrate every one.

MONDAY, 11 JUNE 2012

WHAT DOESN'T KILL YOU MAKES YOU STRONGER

TODAY I MANAGED 7.5KM ON THE BIKE!! It's great because it means that my energy levels are coming back!! It's crazy to think that exactly six weeks ago I was getting out of hospital with only enough energy to walk from my bed to the couch, only retreating back to bed when it was time to sleep, and trying for a nap on the couch during the afternoon.

On Thursday I went up to Auckland to the surgeon who said my leg is progressing well, which is exciting. Then we had lunch with one of our great family friends. After that, I had to have a nap — and in the evening we went to LADY GAGA!!! She had a five-level castle, more costume changes than you could count, and was an amazing performer. How does she dance and sing like that for two and a half hours? It made me tired just watching her. I spent the next two days in Auckland catching up with friends.

On Sunday, as I have done for many years, I went to see the Warren Miller ski movie with the Walshes. When I was younger I used to look at these movies and dream about being in them — impossible, really, because they feature the best skiers in the world. But it made me realise I can never do that now, and never ski like that ever, and that sucked.

Some dreams like skiing in a Warren Miller film or sailing in the Volvo Ocean Race probably never would have come true, but it's hard to realise that I am physically never going to be able to complete those dreams … I guess this gives way to new dreams.

SIX WEEKS AGO
HOW I AM NOW
WOULD HAVE SEEMED
LIKE A DREAM.

My dreams have changed through this whole experience, it's not that I have lost my old ones. I still would like to work for the UNHCR at some point in my life. I still want to help people. And I have new dreams like dancing with Anthony when he comes back from Dunedin, or meddling in Toby's love life, or just having lunch with Kate … but more than anything I want to stay cancer-free.

SATURDAY, 16 JUNE 2012

A LITTLE KINDNESS

IT'S NOT HARD TO COMMIT A RANDOM ACT OF KINDNESS. When I was at Lady Gaga, I saw two Japanese ladies in the seats in front of me who had on the coolest coloured wigs that I had ever seen. While we were waiting for Lady Gaga to go on, I asked where they had got their wigs from, and they replied that they had got them from Japan.

I thought that this would be the end of our conversation but these lovely ladies came up to me after the show and asked me what my address was, as they would like to send me their wigs. This was such an unexpected kindness — the women did not know me from a dot. I found it amazing they would choose to go out of their way for a stranger.

THESE WOMEN SHOW
WHAT EXTRAORDINARY
PEOPLE LIVE ON
THIS EARTH.

One of the gorgeous pink wigs that arrived in the mail.

P.S. Happy Birthday, Jannie. I love you to the moon and back! xoxo

FRIDAY, 22 JUNE 2012

TO BE HUMAN

I AM NO LONGER AN ALIEN. I no longer have probes sticking out of me!!! Today, my Hickman line was taken out. Today, I took a step forward to being a normal teenager once again. I ended up having to have surgery to get it out, but it is finally done, and I am so happy!

It is a big step, as it means that my blood counts are returning to normal. My parents are really excited by this. For me it is just another thing I had to do on the way to getting better. What's more exciting for me is the feeling I had when I stayed over at a friend's place on Sunday. We were sitting in the lounge and everyone was taking the piss out of me for being so spoilt, keeping me grounded as only good friends can, and I was hogging the couch … when I realised something, I didn't feel like a sick kid at all. I felt like a normal teenager hanging out with her mates.

It's not that I mind talking about being sick because it is part of who I am, and what my life is based around at the moment. It is more that whenever I left hospital I would feel great because I would be healthier than most of the people on the ward, but as soon as I returned home I would realise how sick I still was compared to a normal person. I don't feel that anymore. I don't feel like I am on the *same* level yet, but I am no longer looking up as if their level of health is a million times higher than mine.

I'M GETTING THERE.

P.S. Happy Birthday, Toby. Thank you for always being there, whether it was bringing me my cheeseburgers, or putting up with my bad jokes — and just being a generally amazing friend.

THURSDAY, 5 JULY 2012

A HAPPY FREAK

So life is better than amazing right now. Last week most of my friends came back to Wellington. I was busy morning until night, and then into the early hours of the dawn. Dad almost killed me when he got my food bill for last week. I am lucky he loves me so.

Right now, I am writing from my room in the gorgeous Sea Temple Resort in Port Douglas. Mum and Dad really pushed the boat out and this place is FANCY. I feel properly spoiled. It's a poolside apartment: swim-in-swim-out!

As you can probably tell I am incredibly white. I was almost translucent when I got here, but hopefully it is slowly going. What this means is I have to be onto it with the sunblock. No more cancer for me. Hopefully!

It's been a bit strange going out so much. I forgot how different I look to everyone else. It's funny because I quite often catch people staring, and I wonder what I look like to someone who doesn't know. Do I still look sick?

I would have thought that I wouldn't still feel like the sick kid now, but I do. No, it's not so much 'sick' but 'invalid'. My leg feels different. It's like it knows that there is something foreign in it, something not right, and it doesn't want to work as well as it did.

Which doesn't stop me acting like a teenager again! I went to parties on Friday and Saturday, and was able to stand for long periods and even dance! I think the fact that I was rather intoxicated helped me not to notice.

Last week I even managed to go shopping with my friend. I walked for forty-five minutes as well as trying on clothes! And I found a dress which made me feel pretty, which is really hard. As much as I try to pretend it doesn't bother me, my appearance depresses me. I look so abnormal — and at 18, appearance is a big part of who you are. My appearance has changed, and it's hard, because it means every time I look in the mirror I am reminded that I am a freak. Different.

To be fair, I am a happy freak. I am healthy and lapping up the sun in Port Douglas! I am going to visit crocodiles and snakes tomorrow and, if I am really lucky, I might even cuddle a koala! I am a happy freak.

A happy freak I am.

My pretty!

MONDAY, 16 JULY 2012

A CONFUSED WORKING GIRL

TODAY I OFFICIALLY BECAME A WORKING GIRL!! Or a volunteering girl. I have come to the end of my constant lunching and brunching. This is amazing. I am volunteering at the Plimmerton School library helping out the librarian Fiona with anything and everything.

It feels good to be useful again. It also makes the time when I am not working feel more like down time, making it more special. I went for my first trip to the Porirua pool today. I managed to swim a measly six lengths before retiring to the spa, but as the weather was so grot outside, the spa was actually rather lovely!

I have been keeping myself busy and, I am sure, annoying my friends to the brink of insanity. One night I was at a mate's flat and some guy who I hardly know said to me, 'Why do you always talk about cancer? It's over, and it's kinda depressing that you always talk about it.'

These weren't his actual words but the general gist of what he was asking me. It got me thinking, do I talk about cancer too much? Am I obsessed? Is it really over???

I asked two of my friends if they thought I talked about it too much. One said yes, one said no.

I don't think I am obsessed, and I think maybe it is over for everyone else but not for me. I also realise that it's such a big part of my life — *everything* in my life for the past year has centered around it. But what to do?

I don't want people to feel uncomfortable around me because I am talking about cancer all the time, but I still want people to feel comfortable asking questions if they want to. Maybe time will mean it is less of a presence in my life, and more things will take centre stage. Being a working girl is just another step to becoming normal again.

THURSDAY, 9 AUGUST 2012

SCARFIE FOR A WEEK

LAST WEEK I TURNED INTO A SCARFIE who awkwardly had no scarf — as I forgot it. That's right! I braced the cold and saw my friends in Dunedin, and what a wonderful week it was. I have not been as happy in the longest time.

I arrived on Wednesday 25 July and stayed until Wednesday 1 August!!! I had the most amazing time running around and seeing where everyone lived and catching up with them!! I went out for the most fabulous meals, saw the most amazing people and even had a shot of Midori while partying with the cook!!

I almost felt like a normal teenager again. I still have a long way to go — I occasionally need naps in the afternoon and my leg hurts if I push it too far — but life is looking up. I cannot wait until it's me at university.

I used to have trouble even imagining my life would be like it is now. Everything is happening so quickly, and time is seemingly flying by. I have been back for over a week (I needed a wee bit of recovery time!) — but it only seems like I just got back.

It's nearly my birthday, too, which means that it's nearly a year since all of this started. I was diagnosed on 25 August last year, the day before my birthday, and in sixteen days it will be my anniversary of living with cancer. 1/19 of my life.

It feels like a lifetime ago that I was a normal 18-year-old. I don't think I ever will be normal again. I think this will affect me for the rest of my life. Not just physically, with things like not being able to play sports and being limited with movement, but mentally. Cancer will always be a part of me.

As I move further on I make new memories that don't relate to cancer. It will always be there, but there *is* life afterwards, and those who judge me for having it don't matter, and those who don't judge me do.

I love working at the library because the kids don't care about anything like that — not what you look like, just if you are nice or not. It also supplies great entertainment. Today a little boy came into the library crying, apparently some girl had given him a hug and he had girl cooties, which were incurable. He said this as he was hugging me. That's when he looked up and said, 'Oh no — you're a girl too!' and howled harder.

THANKFULLY CANCER IS NOT CONTAGIOUS
BUT OBVIOUSLY GIRL COOTIES ARE.

The lovely Sarah, Kate and I had a girls' night in watching *Finding Nemo* and having a cheeky few. The blue things are shark lollies because obviously they wanted to go swimming! Me (left), Sarah (right).

The QMC girly dinner!!

MONDAY, 13 AUGUST 2012

HOW A HAIRCUT CAN HURT

MILEY CYRUS IS SUCH A BEAUTIFUL GIRL. No matter what you think of her music, this is a fact. At the moment all over Facebook are pictures of her 'radical' new haircut. It hurts me seeing the comments that some people are making about her.

Miley Cyrus is a stunning girl who rocks short hair or long hair. I, on the other hand, am very ordinary. When someone who looks like she does is called 'ugly', 'a butch-looking dyke', 'dumbf**k' and so many more names … it shouldn't hurt me, but it does.

IS THAT WHAT PEOPLE THINK OF ME
WHEN I WALK ALONG THE STREET?

If someone who looks like her can't be considered beautiful with short hair, what are the chances that I can?

I find it difficult to accept the way I look because it has changed so much, but how can I like how I look if nobody else does?

FRIDAY, 31 AUGUST 2012

THE LONGEST YEAR OF MY LIFE

I'M NOT KIDDING WHEN I SAY it has been THE longest year of my life. Not one other year has had such lows or has changed me so much. It has now been one year since I was diagnosed. I cannot believe one year has come and gone. It feels like a lifetime ago that I was a normal teenager with hair and just a sore knee.

I sent the year off in style with an awesome party and copious amounts of drinking and dancing. It was the best way I could imagine to finish a horrible year and set the scene for what is to come — and, oh, are there ever things to come.

Today, I went to the Victoria University open day. It was such a nice day and it made me look forward to next year. It sounds so interesting and exciting, but it's also getting closer to the time that I am going travelling!!!

I have booked a Contiki tour, which is UBER exciting! I am going with my lovely friend Steven Petris who is one of the most lovely friends I could have asked for. He, however, will murder me for giving away that he is secretly a wonderful person. I'm going away for three months, leaving in twenty-three days!!!

Before I can even contemplate that, I am going to Auckland to visit the surgeon, Christchurch to visit my friends down there, and Hawkes Bay to stay with my Grandma. Life is going once again at a fast pace, and I could not be happier.

I am healthy and I am happy and it's amazing … not to wake up every day and want to vomit, not to walk up the stairs and need a sleep … even having enough energy to have a shower is a massive achievement.

Not everything is perfect, but it's so much better that I really cannot complain. I truly am blessed with a great bunch of friends and an amazing family. Speaking of which, my amazing cousins all came to stay for my birthday! Don't they look dashing???

THURSDAY, 4 OCTOBER 2012

UP, UP AND AWAY

Sorry I haven't updated this in a while. I was so preoccupied with getting ready to go to Chicago and saying goodbye to friends, which I admit is a little overdramatic as I am only really gone for two weeks … for now, anyway!

I find it difficult to say 'I had cancer', as it still feels very real to me. But starting out on my journey, I feel I am truly beginning a new sort of chapter in my life. Not to say I am leaving my old life behind — rather, I am creating new beginnings in a life forever changed.

Anyway, the more I've thought about it the more I think that I should start a new blog and leave this one for cancer-related purposes. My experience with the dog is much more sporadic and not consuming my life now, as I start to move in different and exciting directions.

Naming this new blog was a difficult thing for me to do. Much harder than *My Experience of Walking the Dog*. I think it's because I have had more time to mull it over and thus more naming options.

However I have decided to call it *Plan B*. As my life is 'Plan B'. It's not turned out how it was supposed to go, and it will never be what it used to be, but that's okay. Different is not a bad thing. The link to the blog is at the bottom of this page. Luckily the test results I had before I went away were still according to plan, and showed me to be in the All Clear! However I had to have THREE of my immunizations again in ONE day. My arm was sore for a week after.

I am lucky that the only sickness I have had recently is a sore arm and a cold. It's makes for a nice change of pace!

Check out my new blog at:

THELIFEOFPLANB.BLOGSPOT.COM

FRIDAY, 19 OCTOBER 2012

BATTLE SCARS

I HAVE BATTLE SCARS that I will have to live with. Today I am leaving to begin a new chapter in my story. I am going away travelling for two and a half months by MYSELF!!

Today is not as stressful as I thought it would be. I have packed everything and am ready to leave. I will miss Mum and Dad but I think that it is important for me to do this. It is a big step in regaining my independence and confidence.

Poor Dad and Mum, though. At this point in time I am healthier than my doctors hoped I would be, but I am also not as healthy as Mum and Dad would have wanted me to be. I still get tired, and I still have trouble walking long distances and standing up for long periods of time.

I went and saw the physio on Tuesday and he said that my leg has reached a plateau. I still can't really bend it 90° which means that I will always have trouble going up and down stairs, but today is a beautiful day in which I set off on a brand new chapter.

THE BATTLE SCARS THAT I HAVE
ARE PART OF WHO I AM, BUT
THEY DO NOT DEFINE ME.

PLAN B — THE LIMITED EDITION

A GIRL I WENT TO SCHOOL WITH said flippantly to one of my close friends, 'I used to read Harriet's blog every day until I found out that she was going to survive, then it got boring.' So of course this information was rushed back to me. At the time I was flabbergasted and a little hurt. Then I realised that all I had written about since getting better was my travels.

So I decided I would cut those posts down for this book. Also, I don't want anyone getting bored halfway through just because I talked about my adventures. I have to face the simple fact that although people like scandalous stories and tragedies, they find hearing about other people's holidays rather boring, especially if they're as long as mine. I cannot fault this.

If I got asked to read someone's three-month travel diary, I probably wouldn't be that interested either. So what I will write for you here is a very condensed version of my Plan B blog.

My life at this stage was not what I expected it to be. I was better than I had been a few months before — although still not quite running or jumping — but these three months were three of the best I have ever had.

There was no way I was not going travelling. When I had to have many a nasty needle or other medical device poking or prodding me, I was told stories of where I was going on my fabulous world trip: the Trip of a Lifetime. They kept me going.

Mum always said that if she wrote a blog she'd be useless because she would write in bullet points. So I thought this was a good plan to show you how amazing my trip was without going into heaps of detail.

1. Chicago
2. Abu Dhabi
3. London
4. Croatia
5. Bosnia and Herzegovina — where I slipped and hurt my knee.
6. Croatia
7. London — where I found out that I had broken my kneecap in Bosnia and Herzegovina.
8. *Not* Amsterdam — because my **** knee kept me in London (so I missed the beginning of the Contiki tour). Yay! Got the leg cast taken off, and caught the next flight out to Berlin after taking a quick day trip to:
9. Brighton

10. Berlin — where my friend Rike picked me up and looked after me for the night until my Contiki group caught up!

On crutches, travelled with my Contiki group to:

11. Munich
12. Venice
13. Rome
14. Florence
15. Lucerne
16. Paris — which ended my Contiki. N.B. Mini stops included the Leaning Tower of Pisa, Dresden and a few other cities along the way!
17. Zurich
18. Milan and Lake Como (a beautiful Italian lake) — a road trip with Jannie.
19. Zurich — where my mother flew in to meet me and took me off to:
20. Morocco — which isn't actually as nice as you think it would be. We were meant to be there for three weeks, but Mum got sick, and after ten days we'd had enough so we went to:
21. Barcelona — which we loved, but Mum was so sick :(
22. London — for Christmas.
23. Little old Wellington, New Zealand — returning on New Years Eve.

I must say I had the most fantastic and ridiculously amazing time. I travelled thinking the cancer was gone and was never coming back. I made friends, did amazing things and saw incredible places — as I planned to do for the rest of my life.

I'd spent most of the previous year in a hospital bed and needed to live every second as if it was my last. I know you can't always count on a future. I had to live for the 'now' and make sure I didn't ever have an 'I wish' or 'why didn't I?' thought.

And I certainly don't.

PLAN B WAS MY LIFE AFTER CANCER.

IT'S FUNNY HOW PLANS CHANGE.

67

SATURDAY, 16 FEBRUARY 2013

THE HARDEST THING I WILL EVER SAY

I HAVE PUT OFF WRITING THIS and I keep on justifying it to myself by making multiple different excuses, but the main reason I haven't written is because I do not want to. I never wanted to tell anyone this, or to put my family through it, but like a lot of things, I haven't really got a choice.

On 13 February I went and had a CT scan which showed that I have tumours covering my entire lungs. This basically looks like the end of the road for me.

I wish I had better news to tell you but it's got about as bad as cancers get.

On the upside I am moving into my hall in a week! I have loads of things to look forward to. I refuse to give up. I am going to keep living life to its fullest until I simply can't anymore.

Don't feel too sorry for me. I have had a fabulous life and everybody has to die at some point, and who knows I might even make it to 20! I have been extremely lucky. I have had my family who adore and love me more than I deserve. I have better friends than anybody I know. I could not have asked for a better bunch. I have been to amazing places and done amazing things and lived with no real regrets.

This way I will NEVER have to get a job, learn how to cook more than two-minute noodles or do anything mildly productive. I never have to grow up and I can forever be a kid! Though my 'forever' is shorter than most, I don't mind. What I do mind is that I am going to have to leave everyone I love behind.

The people I love are amazing and I am so sorry for doing this to you.

I AM SO VERY SORRY.

I LOVE YOU.

'MY THOUGHTS ARE
STARS I CANNOT
FATHOM INTO
CONSTELLATIONS.'

THE FAULT IN
OUR STARS
JOHN GREEN

SUNDAY, 3 MARCH 2013

LIVING MY LIFE

My life, like most, has its ups and downs. I try to stay positive and most of the time I succeed. This week has been amazingly bittersweet! I am loving living in the hall, but at the same time it sucks that I don't have the same energy levels as everyone else here.

I have loved and hated making new friends. I have loved meeting these new amazing people, but at the same time I know that I am only going to hurt them. This week I have had some of the best times I have ever had, but I have also had some of the worst.

I went to see Anne who, as usual, was super amazing. I just wished she'd had better news. The cancer has spread so far in my lungs that they cannot surgically operate and leave me with enough functioning lung to live.There is no way for me ever to be cancer-free, but that's ok. This is my lot and I am okay with it. I just need to have the most fun I possibly can until it happens. To end this on a positive note, I will add a photo of getting ready for the toga party! Such fun!

WEDNESDAY, 6 MARCH 2013

THANKS!

I JUST WANTED TO WRITE A BIG THANKS (I am in my study break/procrastinating/starting my readings) to the people who have been dropping off or sending gifts to Boulcott Hall for me:) It has been ever so lovely to receive packages reminding me of how much support I have.

I honestly could not ask for better friends. I know it's been really hard for so many of you, and I am really sorry for that. People tell me I should stop apologising because it's not my fault. I know this, but I still feel bad for putting everybody through it. When I die, I won't have to deal with the grief and loss you all do. I will never be able to say 'thank you' or 'sorry' enough. I love you all.

ON A HAPPIER NOTE, ENJOY A PICTURE OF THE AMAZING CUPCAKES I HAD THE PLEASURE OF DEVOURING!!

FRIDAY, 22 MARCH 2013

GOODY TWO SHOES

I AM OVERLY CHUFFED WITH MYSELF at the moment because I got my first grades back, and I am officially a straight A student! I got two marks back, and managed to get an A– and an A+!

I am actually so proud! I don't know how long I will be able to stay at uni or even how long I will live, but I can honestly say that I am living my life to the fullest. I know the idea that going to live in a hall and eating hall food (euch! SAVE ME!!!), and going to uni and doing work is not what everyone would choose to do if they only had six months to live, but it makes me so happy.

I miss my family. It's hard not living with them, especially since I know how difficult they're finding this — and I love them so very much — but I am doing something which I have dreamed about for so long.

I know it's not forever. I can feel it getting harder all the time. I also know that my grades don't really matter because I probably won't even finish first year, but for now, I am a student.

AND I ABSOLUTELY LOVE IT.

FRIDAY, 29 MARCH 2013

HAPPINESS COMES IN MANY FORMS

I NEVER THOUGHT I WOULD BE HAPPY being told I have six more months to live, but strangely I am. I got scans taken on Wednesday and the results are in and they are good. They are not 'you are going to live' good, but that was never really a choice. At this point, going from my first appointment where they guessed I would have around six months, that could mean I have only three to four months left.

Yet the tumours have hardly grown. They *have* grown, as that is the nature of cancer, but they haven't grown that much. I have been told that although this still only gives me months, it means that I have more time to spend being happy and healthy!!

I am actually able to hope that I will see my brother turn 18, and I may even get to turn 20!!! I no longer have to be some annoying teen. I sometimes forget that the news isn't as exciting for everyone else, as I still die at the end of this. But it is one of the biggest gifts I could have been given: more time. I am going to use it wisely.

Dad has booked a family holiday. In just under three weeks I am going to Verona, Paris and Amsterdam. I am going to the Anne Frank House. This may sound slightly morbid, and I guess it is. I sometimes forget how much I have changed since I turned 18. I know it made me grow up fast. I understand that, but what I sometimes forget is how morbid it makes me. I don't talk about death knowingly but it is such a constant presence that I forget that it is not normal for most people. Sometimes I feel a bit lonely, because I don't really know anyone who has been in this situation.

This is why I fell in love with the book *The Fault in Our Stars* by John Green. It's such a wonderful book, about somebody who has cancer. It is probably the truest book on how it really feels.

Hazel Grace and Augustus Waters, although they are only made-up characters, are my friends, and they help me through this. Hazel Grace falls in love with a book (book-ception, methinks) and it makes her want to go to Amsterdam, and while she is there she goes to the Anne Frank House. This spectacular book made me want to do the exact same thing.

This may not seem like a miracle, but having more time — and being healthy for just a few more months — is more than I could have hoped for. So Happy Easter!! Spend time with those you love, cherish them, because everyday is precious.

TUESDAY, 14 MAY 2013

MY MONTH OF FUN!!!

It's been odd. Normally I always love writing on my blog — it's a way in which I sort out the things that are rolling around in my mind — but lately I haven't felt the need to. Things have seemed simpler. They are obviously more complicated — but simpler at the same time.

It's simple, I am dying, there is no changing this fact, so if something makes me happy I have been doing it. I've been having so much fun! I drove up to Hobbiton with my friend Hannah and met her family — they are sooo nice and cool. I have been living in my hall, enjoying time at university and being with my amazing friends. And I went to Europe to spend time in Verona, Venice, Milan, Zurich, Paris and Amsterdam!

I have been eating AMAZING, out-of-this-world food and spending some amazing time with some wonderful people. I am actually really happy. I have moments when it hits me and I have a small breakdown, but sometimes I am able to forget what is going on.

The other day I said to my dad, 'Life could not be more perfect.' And his retort was simple, 'It really could be.' And it could. But I am truly happy with my lot in life. It may not be perfect but it's pretty darn good. My energy levels are slowly getting worse, but I have good days and bad. Mum and Dad are still holding strong on the puppy debate. I hope you enjoy these photos of the past month as much as I do!!

At Hobbiton.

Cute night in Boulcott.

Verona! with Dad.

Our apartment in Verona.

Tom, me & Mum.

My favourite dessert ever!

The Fam Bam in the Piazza San Marco.

TUESDAY, 14 MAY 2013

TO HAZEL GRACE

TODAY I WENT TO THE ANNE FRANK HOUSE and I seriously think that this deserves its own blog. It deserves everything. When I planned my trip away, the place I most wanted to go was Amsterdam — to the Anne Frank House. One of my treasured things in this life are books. Anne Frank's diary is a spectacular book, but the book which made me want to go to the Anne Frank House was *The Fault in Our Stars* by John Green.

I know I go on about this book but it's simply because I love it. I know of nobody who is like me. Nobody except Hazel Grace. I know it's not real because she is a fictional character in a book — but for somebody who isn't dying, John Green has created a realistic girl with cancer who reminds me that I am not the only person like me. It makes me both sad and happy. I would love for there to be nobody like me, for nobody else to have to go through this, but they do — and sometimes it's nice to know you are not alone.

The Anne Frank House is an amazing place: sad, haunting, tiny — but amazing. It's painful to see what she had to endure, and a reminder that there are people in this world who have had it worse than me. It was amazing to spend this time with my family and Jannie. They truly are an amazing bunch.

TO MY IMAGINARY FRIENDS
ANNE FRANK & HAZEL GRACE,
THANKS FOR TEACHING ME
HOW TO BE STRONG
AND FOR REMINDING ME
THAT I AM NOT ALONE.

TUESDAY, 14 MAY 2013

DOGS & OTHER BORING STUFF

IT'S GETTING HARDER TO POST ON HERE. Nothing bad is happening, it's just getting harder to live my normal day-to-day life, and that is something which is hard to tell people. It doesn't matter how strong I am or how hard I try to fight this, I cannot win.

It is getting worse and worse and it sucks. The biggest problem that I am having at the moment is with tiredness. Tiredness is something that everyone has to deal with, but it's something nobody truly understands because tiredness doesn't cover it. I am exhausted, constantly.

It means that I go to sleep exhausted, and I wake up exhausted, and there is nothing I can do to change this. It's worse than that. I am starting to struggle with concentration. So I have decided to stop doing my uni work and just go to the lectures, as it's too difficult to concentrate anymore.

I am also more emotional than I normally am, and this messes with me. I am not an emotional person, but recently I have started being really upset for no reason and snapping, and then all of a sudden having a 180° shift and giggling or talking nonsensically … and it's just getting harder to do simple things like get ready.

I struggle, but there is nothing I can do to change any of the above apart from profusely apologise to those I live with, especially to Guy and Hannah who bear the brunt of most of the emotional stuff! I wish I could say it was going to get better but I know it won't. It's only going to get worse.

LUCKILY, DOGS EXIST.

SUNDAY, 26 MAY 2013

A LIVING GRENADE

Grenades are completely harmless until somebody pulls the pin. Once the pin is pulled they cause nothing but pain and sadness. I walk around knowing that at some point soon the pin will be pulled, and all who are near me will be hurt.

Yet knowing this, I continue to draw more people near. This is perhaps the most selfish thing I can do, yet I still do it. When people ask me if I am scared of dying I can honestly reply 'not really'. I am more worried about what it will do to those I love. Hazel Grace said it first, 'I'm a grenade and at some point I'm going to blow up and I would like to minimize the casualties, okay?'

No, I am not an inanimate object like a grenade, I am a particular brand of destruction more like a Venus flytrap. The people who care for me most will be those who are hurt, although even an unlucky passerby may be drawn in too.

I am struggling with this at the moment. I am at a stage in my life where I meet new people all of the time, and it's hard because, although I really want to get to know them, it sometimes scares me. By befriending them, I will knowingly hurt them, but my friends say they would rather have me in their lives and get hurt than not to have me at all. How do I make that call? How do I decide if being my friend will outweigh the hurt and sadness they will one day have to face?

My friend Sarah showed me a quote from a woman who was dying of cancer. When asked, 'What's it like to be dying?' Her response was, 'What's it like pretending you're not?'

I guess in life we are all going to hurt people whether we mean to or not. I may be a live grenade … but so is everyone.

I CAN'T DO
ANYTHING TO STOP THE HURT
I AM GOING TO INFLICT,
BUT I AM SORRY.

SO VERY SORRY.

WEDNESDAY, 5 JUNE 2013

GYM BUNNY

I DO NOT UNDERSTAND GYMS. Seriously, the idea of running when you are not chasing/being chased is ridiculous! What makes it even more ridiculous is that you don't even move, so it's not like you get some well-deserved treat at the end. Yet somehow I have found myself as a member of one.

Actually I know exactly how I came to this: 'doctors' orders'. Sometimes I enjoy doctors' orders. Anne says I am to eat whatever I feel like and not worry about calories. I like these orders even if I was already doing this. I am also supposed to be doing fifteen minutes relaxed exercise a day. This is not bad either — especially since I love swimming!

I am now a member of Habit gym, and I went swimming there for the first time today! It is actually really relaxing. I do especially enjoy lounging in the spa afterwards. Maybe it's lucky I am dying otherwise I would become the fattest person alive!!! Maybe people should run even if they are not being chased.

OR THEY COULD GET A DOG.
THEN THEY COULD WALK THE DOG.

MONDAY, 10 JUNE 2013

A LITTLE DREAM OF MINE

THERE ARE SOME THINGS IN THIS LIFE I will never truly understand, and how we let others kill themselves through lack of knowledge is one of them. This week Boulcott has been doing fundraising for the 40 Hour Famine.

It makes me so sad to think about it. I know more than most that dying sucks. There is nothing I can do to change the fact that I am dying. Absolutely nothing. Yet there are so many people out there dying from things which are curable, and that sucks. I have had so much love in my life, so much happiness. I have been unbelievably lucky to have lived in the time I have, yet I hate the fact that I will never grow old. I accept that this is the way it has to be but I desperately wish it wasn't.

I had really big dreams. I really wanted to become a humanitarian aid worker, and trust me when I say this is not an easy field to get into. I had a five-year plan which listed ways in which I could achieve this goal. I won't bore you with the details, because the fact is it will never be a reality. It will forever just be a dream of what my future could have been. I know that writing a blog entry isn't really a big deal, but in some small way by doing it — even though this is sort of preachy (sorry!) — I feel I am able to help people, and that is all I ever wanted to do.

FRIDAY, 14 JUNE 2013

THE MOST SPECTACULAR SURREAL DAY

THIS WEEK I HAVE HAD one of the most utterly incredible days of my entire life. It was stupendous, rapturous and multiple-other-exuberant adjectives. It was a simply wonderful day. Sometimes I sit around and wonder if this is how I should be spending the last of my life, and then days like this remind me that I am incredibly lucky. I may be dying but 98% of the time I am incredibly happy, and this day was definitely among one of my happiest.

So now to tell you about this frabjous day! Callooh! Callay! My friend Hannah and I had the astounding privilege of being taken onto the set of *The Hobbit* by the wonderful Philippa Boyens. I got to see some amazing sets and meet some amazing people. It was surreal. Truly a day I will never forget.

As Hazel Grace would say, 'BEST CANCER PERK EVER!!!' However the set of *The Hobbit* is tippy-top secret and even if I tried I couldn't describe how unbelievable my day was. Oh wait! I guess I do have a photo with Orlando Bloom and Evangeline Lilly!

FRIDAY, 21 JUNE 2013

THE MARVELLOUS CANTEEN CANCER PERK

THE AMOUNT OF HAPPINESS IN MY LIFE IS RIDICULOUS. At precisely two seconds ago I decided I would never sleep again as I don't want to miss out on any of the happiness that could possibly occur while I am asleep. I realised this was ridiculous after thinking it. I understand pain and sadness but I also understand happiness. I, very fortunately, experience a lot of it.

My memory is shocking — I mean, BAD! So I carry around this little notebook in which I organise my life, and by this I generally mean my social life. Just looking at it shows how much happiness and love I have in my life.

EVERY DAY THERE IS SOME PERSON TO SEE,
SOMETHING TO DO, SOME WONDER WHICH IS TO HAPPEN.

This week on Thursday I had yet another cancer perk. This time it was CanTeen that was the generous organiser. CanTeen has a palliative care grant. It's for kids dying of cancer to create memories — and who doesn't want more wonderful memories?

When I was in Amsterdam on my bucket list trip, I wandered past a shop which was about two doors down from our apartment, and there was this dress. It was simply there waiting for me. The lovely Jannie agreed, and gave it to me, and the dress and I have been inseparable ever since.

The problem I found with this fabulous dress was that it was so 1920s it was almost costume-y. So in true 'me' style, I decided I would have to create events I could wear it to. Lucky for me *The Great Gatsby* movie is out. I decided with the palliative grant money I would make my friends dress up in 1920s fashion, and we'd have a lunch at my favourite restaurant then watch *The Great Gatsby.*

It was an unbelievably wonderful day combing through delicious food with glorious company while wearing a simply spectacular dress. And just to add to the unbelievableness of the day, I now have a good sibling photo!

THURSDAY, 18 JULY 2013

LA DOLCE VITA

Tom, my brother, eighteen?? This doesn't seem possible. Just a few short months ago I was not even sure I was going to be alive let alone healthy and happy!

My six-month deadline is sneaking closer and closer, yet somehow I am still alive and kicking. I blame my family and friends for making my life so wonderful. How am I meant to die when my life is so unbelievably amazing? The last month has been crazily busy but in the best possible way!!

I flew down to Wanaka and spent a week with Zoe and Jackie. We had the most wonderful time of rest and relaxation, and I munched through copious amounts of scrumptious food. In Wellington, not only did I have all my family come for a weekend, I also had my room-mate from Contiki and another friend fly down and spend the week with me! It was so amazing to be reunited.

I even went with my friend Sophie to hold her hand while she got a tattoo. Although I think I ended up being more of a hindrance than a help, as she was as cool as ice while I was having mild panic attacks — and she was the one getting the tattoo!!!

Benedict Cumberbatch & me.

Richard Armitage & me.

Finally, I got to go to the premiere of *The World's End* and walk the red carpet. Yes, you did read that right! Bex and I were invited by the lovely Philippa Boyens to go with her to the premiere — a fabulous excuse to get another lovely dress. It was so cool! We got to meet so many amazing people and see a side-splittingly hilarious film.

It was a surreal experience because nights like that don't happen to people like me! It was one of the most magical nights of my life.

I am so healthy now, I am actually able to plan things in the not-so-distant future. Like next week I am going to Bali, I am going to Beyoncé on 19 October, and I am even able to start thinking about what I'm going to do for my birthday. I am planning on turning 20! N.B. It's on 26 August, just in case you want to start shopping for my present.

AHHHH! It's all ever so exciting! I am also still able to live in the hall and go to university and participate in O Week events (even if Vic Uni puts on the most pathetic O Week events).

LIFE IS SIMPLY SWELL!!

Being clichéd tourists!

Zoe & me in Wanaka.

Cousins.

The lovely Philippa & me before we head off to the premiere.

Bex & me all ready to go!

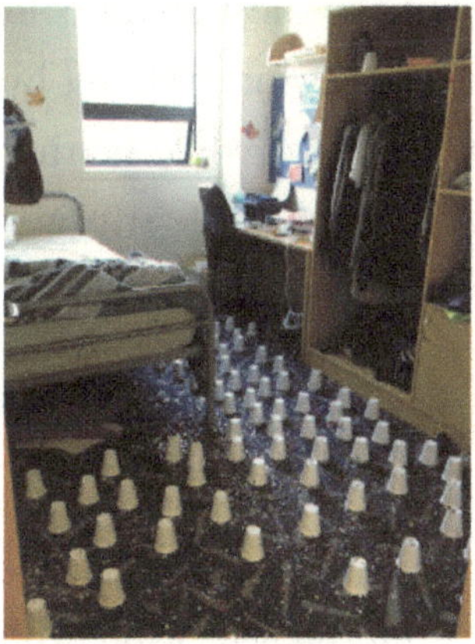

Every single one of those cups is filled with confetti.

Problem: when you pick up the cup the confetti goes everywhere!

TUESDAY, 6 AUGUST 2013

HIGHS & LOWS

SOMEBODY ONCE TOLD ME that the hardship we experience in our life makes us appreciate the good times even more. In most respects this is true, but living through the lows still sucks.

The last two weeks have been a roller coaster. Last week I went to Bali with my family and had one of the best weeks of my life. I had the most awful cold when I went over there, so there was lots of lying by the pool and eating scrumptious food while getting better. I even flew business class. The whole trip was rather swellegant! It was a special week away with three of my favourite people in the world.

Sadly to my high there must be a low. While I was away my nana passed away. My nana was a pretty spectacular person. During her youth she was a dancer and entertained the troops during the war. When she stopped dancing, she decided to take up athletics and competed all around the world. More importantly she was such a nice person.

My nana was not my biological nana but the mother of my old nanny, Pam. She decided to adopt me as a grandchild. For six years I spent at least one afternoon a week with my wonderful nana and granddad. She was always trying to make me fat with delicious home-baked sweets, and even when I couldn't have any more, she'd wrap up a little takeaway bag.

Nana was one of the strongest people I have ever known. She was so determined and threw herself into everything with absolute passion. I'm proud to be her granddaughter and I will miss her greatly. Tomorrow I will borrow a little of the strength she instilled in me and face up to my tests with a smile. No matter what the outcome, I can get through them. I can do it.

Tomorrow I have to have a CT scan to see whether I need radiation. One of the tumours may be too close to my vocal chords, and I could require palliative radiation to keep my voice.

My life is not an easy one but it is mine. I sometimes think I would love to trade lives with anyone, but in fact I wouldn't. I wish that I didn't have cancer, but if I wasn't me then I wouldn't have all these amazing people in my life. My life may not be easy but it is full of love. For that I am thankful.

Bali.

RIP my wonderful nana & granddad.

WEDNESDAY, 7 AUGUST 2013

THE RESULTS SHOW

I'M NOT SURE HOW TO WRITE THIS REALLY because yesterday I went to the hospital and I had both good news and bad. I guess I should start with the good news.

Last time I talked to Anne I thought she suggested radiation to help me keep my voice. Luckily that involved a lot of 'ifs' (which I didn't realise), and *I do not have those ifs*. The tumours are only in my lungs not anywhere else.

Now the not-so-good news. My naughty little tumours aren't so little anymore. They have grown quite a bit since my last X-ray. The biggest one is about five to seven centimetres in diameter, and there are more than twelve others of a significant size. They seem to be growing more quickly now, but I will see in two months when I have my next scans.

So on the plus side, I don't have to have radiation, which is what I was really worried about. I love being a student and having fun, and radiation would have made me so tired. It would have sucked. I wish the tumours were smaller, because we are still only talking about months. Who knows? According to the first prognosis *two years ago* I was given six months to live, and I am sitting on six months now.

I have lots to look forward to! It's my birthday in less than twenty days, which is so exciting!! I never thought I would turn 20!! I am going to the Beyoncé concert with Dad and Tom. I even have my hall ball.

Sometimes when I feel sad I just remember what a good life I have and it helps me. I honestly have had one of the best lives ever, and I fully intend to keep enjoying it.

BRING ON BEING 20!!

THURSDAY, 22 AUGUST 2013

MAKING 20

I'M GOING TO MAKE IT TO 20. I am actually going to turn 20! Monday is so close now! I can almost smell it. At the beginning of this year I was told I only had six months to live. I wondered whether I would get to see Tom turn 18. I didn't even think I could make it to my own 20th!

It makes me smile to think that this is not the end of me, not yet. I have a bit more life in me, a few more memories to make. Who knows what I have left to do. Life will never be perfect, so it's important to appreciate moments and milestones, and this may be one of the happiest milestones I have ever reached.

I have already had some amazing birthday treats, and it's not even my birthday yet. I just have the best friends a girl could ask for.

SOMETIMES I LOVE MY LIFE
BECAUSE, JUST IN CASE
YOU MISSED IT,
I'M STILL ALIVE!!!!

THURSDAY, 5 SEPTEMBER 2013

THE GOOD, THE BAD & THE UGLY

THIS TITLE IS RATHER OVERDRAMATIC, which I sometimes fear is a word that should be applied to me. Overdramatic Harriet. Sometimes I am too. Earlier in the year I fell over and I was certain that I had broken my foot and told everyone so. I hadn't. I am still embarrassed to this day remembering what a drama queen I was about it. But most of the time I like to think I am not.

I have been having a ridiculous amount of fun. I turned 20!! I actually did it!! I'm 20!! This is a huge milestone and I have spent the last two weeks celebrating it. My parents have dubbed it my birthday festival, as I have been so spoiled and been having so much fun with the most wondrous people.

I think I should definitely turn 20 more often. I would recommend it to anyone. It has been the best birthday I have ever had. Jannie even flew in from Zurich to celebrate with me, and people flew in from all over the country. So much delicious food and wonderful people and copious amounts of alcohol. What more could I want?

But like everything you can't have the highs without the lows. Two days ago I felt a sharp pain in the side of my ribcage every time I breathed in. I told myself that I had just pulled a muscle with all my vigorous dancing, but on Sunday night I decided that I couldn't really ignore it anymore and I sent an email to Anne. She replied quickly on Monday morning telling me that it was important that I call her and arrange an appointment.

I awoke to a call from Sophie asking what I was doing as she was on her way over, and was I out of bed yet? I had to confess that her call had woken me. She laughed and told me to get in the shower, and playfully reminded me most people wake up when the clock reads 'am'.

Instead of having a shower like Sophie suggested, I decided to see if Anne had emailed. She had, so I called her and she said that it was important that I come in and we check out what was going on. So, as per usual, when Sophie showed up I was still in my PJs and she had to run me through the motions of getting ready. I was being rather toddler-like, as even though the rational part of me knew I should go, I really didn't want to.

With the help of Sophie and Tessa, I finally got into Will's car. Will had very luckily decided to bring his dog Molly along for the ride, which left me completely and utterly smitten. Molly and I cuddled all the way to the hospital. I cannot describe how gorgeous she is.

When I got to the hospital I started to get nervous again, but as anyone knows in hospitals there is a lot of waiting around. I went and got an X-ray and saw Anne's registrar before they had only done one X-ray rather than two, so I had to go and get another one done. Luckily I had Sophie with me who is rather excellent company and continually makes me laugh.

Both scans showed nothing. So then they became worried that I might have a blood clot in my lungs and they got very worried. Words were being thrown around like 'Clexane injections', which are better known as rat poison. At this point I decided I should tell Mum that I was in hospital.

After much grumbling and being a 'fraidy cat (all on my part) a nurse was able to get a line in, and I headed down to get a CT scan. I even got a ride on a bed they were so worried, with Mum and Soph chuckling all the way and making Princess Harriet jokes. Luckily the CT scan showed that I have no clots — so yay! No rat poison for me!!! One of my little tumours has decided to get an infection around it and attach itself to my lung lining, which is what is causing the pain. Rather annoying. So, hopefully, I will be able to take antibiotics for a week and it will go away. I have an appointment with Anne next week. If it isn't better by then … I will cross that bridge when I get there.

What's been more scary than the hospital visit is the pain. It makes everything so much more real. I do understand what is happening to me, but most of the time I can ignore it, and try to live my life and be as happy as I can be. When you feel pain every time you breathe, it's right there, staring you in the face. There is no way around this. I am dying.

There is not that much time left for me. I don't mean this in the sense that I am dying as we speak, but I mean I don't have years. I have months. One thing that I do is every time I see people I love I try to say, 'I love you'. I don't know how much more I will be able to tell them that.

If this week has shown me anything, it's that I have so many people I love and who love me, and I am going to try to tell them so much as possible.

BECAUSE I DO.
ALWAYS HAVE.
ALWAYS WILL.

Quick trip to hospital with Sophie.

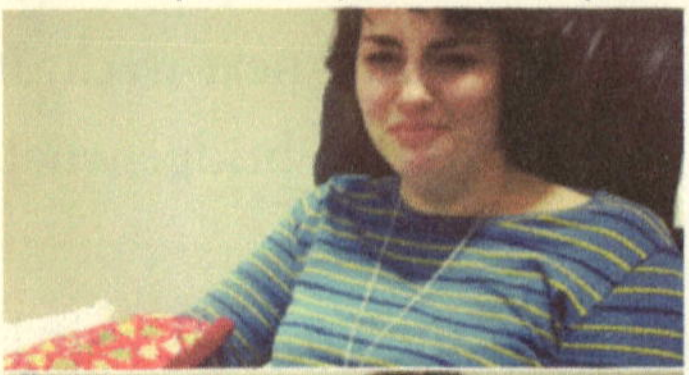

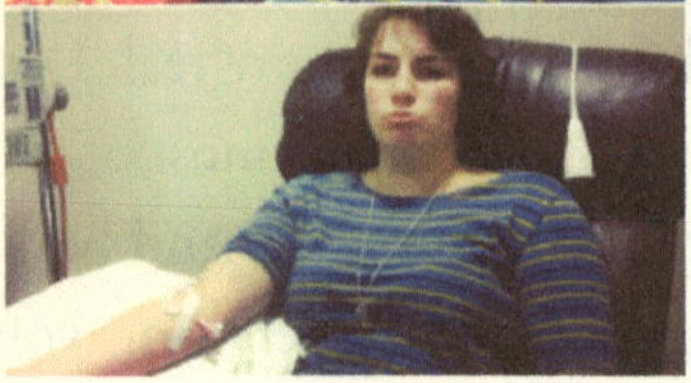

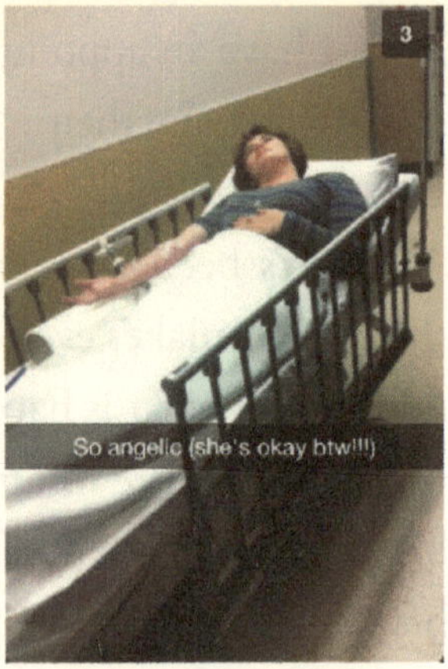

Pizza dinner with
a few friends on my birthday.

Boulcott Gatsby party: I may or may not have picked the theme so I could wear the dress again …

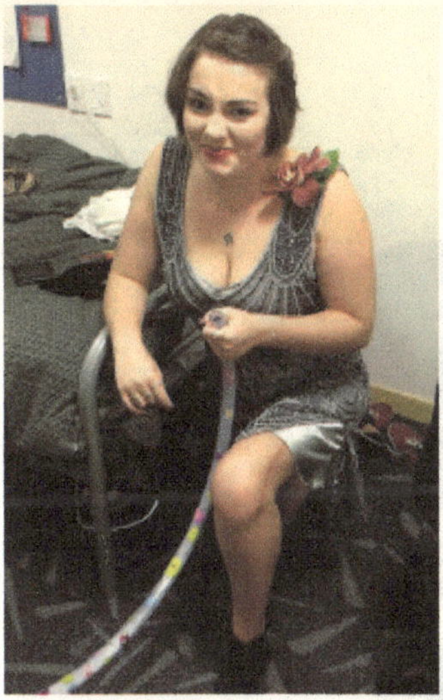

My surprise birthday dinner
with wonderful friends.

I may have missed Tessa slightly.

The spectacular Sophie
who looks after me!

LUCKILY THIS PUP
WAS AROUND FOR CUDDLES!

SADLY, THIS PUPPY IS MY GRANDDAD'S.
I HAVEN'T GOT A PUPPY.

YET.

MONDAY, 16 SEPTEMBER 2013

MOOD SWINGS

THE SADNESS CREEPS UP SLOWLY, sometimes it seems to disappear entirely, but there is always this smidge of sadness which I can't properly shake. I wish I could, but the truth is I am sad. Don't get me wrong. I am happy too, but I am sad. Augustus in *The Fault in Our Stars* said it right when he said:

'The marks humans leave are too often scars.'

Everywhere I look now I seem to be leaving scars and I hate it. I don't want to cause people pain but I don't know how to stop it.

I have reached that point in hyper-exhaustion where my mood swings are involuntary and often uncontrollable. I will get angry for a very small, almost non-existent reason, then feel like crying, and then have fits of uncontrollable laughter.

It is messing with my head. I have never had this little control over my emotions and it scares me. On the plus side I haven't been able to stop eating the past couple of days, which may mean that I truly do end up on the 'plus' side of life.

Life moves on and it continues to move forward, and I have so much to look forward to. I simply wish I had more control, more time, more puppy, more everything really. Especially more puppy. That would be nice. Red pandas too!

SUNDAY, 27 OCTOBER 2013

THE GREAT & THE MISERABLE

SORRY IT'S BEEN SO LONG SINCE I WROTE HERE. Life has been moving quickly! I have almost not stopped moving. I love to keep moving. I am one of those people who gets bored very easily. And I love to be doing things. I'm so lucky that, in the last six weeks, that is basically all I have been doing. It's been crazy!

In the last six weeks I have had my hall ball which was amazing. It was held at Te Papa, and I had such a good night dancing with all my Boulcott kids! I had the most amazing dress, but I don't think Dad really approved. When he saw it he asked me if Miley Cyrus had picked it out ...

I went down to Dunedin to visit all my friends — a pretty spectacular week filled with much lunching and brunching and a little bit of partying. I even managed to fit in a wonderful trip to the butterfly exhibit, and a quick cuddle with my uncle's gorgeous dogs.

I went to Beyoncé in Auckland which was amazing — she is such a superstar! Tom, who doesn't even like her music, had to admit that it was one of the best concerts that he'd ever seen. I may have over-exaggerated it when I said 'the best concert he'd ever seen', but he said it was 'good' and that's about as much as you will ever get him to admit. I think Tom will now secretly sing Beyoncé in the shower when he thinks we can't hear him! Dad loved her more. I was, well ... my normal diva.

I even went to Park Road Post Production and got to see *The Hobbit* being made into the wonderful film it is going to be. I am sooo excited to see the whole thing, but as per usual I can tell you nothing apart from the fact that Philippa Boyens is truly one of the most amazing women I have had the pleasure of meeting.

I have also had Boulcott's end of year events to go to, as we have to move out on 16 November. Everyone is moving into exams, which is CRAZY. I'm obviously studying hard! I am lucky to have lived here, though.

Dinners galore.

Dunedin beach walks.

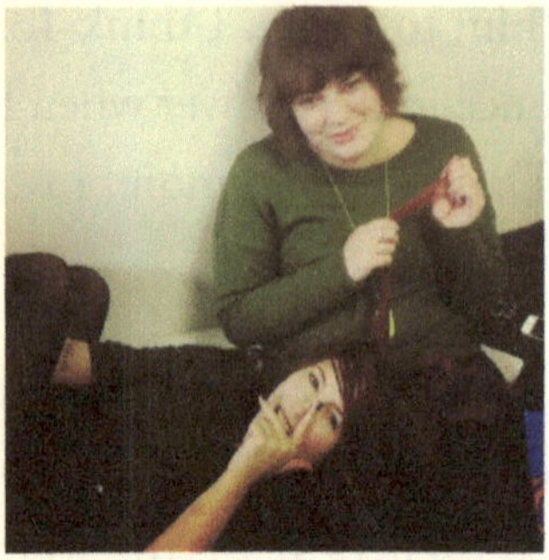

Making Sophie into my ghetto flower.

I have met some of the most amazing people, and I'm so happy that they are in my life. It's such a cool place to live. I absolutely love it.

Over this time, I have also attempted to bake, watched dearest Simon play rugby, and driven to Hawkes Bay and Levin to spend time with my grandparents. I have watched many movies. I have caught up with old friends and made new friends. I have been to plays, and a musical where Anya beguiled the audience.

I have had more brunches, lunches, coffees, dinners, afternoon teas (and any other word you can describe a catch-up revolving around food) than I care to admit! Life has been amazing!

Now for the miserable side of this blog. I have a little tear in my lung and it's bleeding. This is about as much fun as it sounds. I am on some very nice painkillers to get rid of the pain, but there is not much the doctors can really do apart from hope it fixes itself, or maybe give me a small round of steroids. It's making me really tired.

It's so annoying as I still want to do so much, but I have to take it easy and not stress my body out too much (which I am not very good at doing). So I have my fingers crossed that it will get better, but I guess we always knew this was coming. There isn't much that I can do about it so I try not to worry. That's not always possible, but I can try my best.

'That's the thing about pain. It demands to be felt.' My dear John Green. I wish this wasn't the case but like most things he wrote about when he wrote *The Fault in Our Stars*, he is right. Pain sucks and as much as you try to ignore it, it is still there. I'm simply lucky I have such wonderful distractions.

NOT PUPPY-LEVEL
OF DISTRACTION
BUT GOOD ONES
ALL THE SAME.

Hall ball with Eddy & Simon.

Boulcott bingo night.

The wonderful Tessa.

My amazing floor.

We 'B' sad to leave Boulcott.

SATURDAY, 16 NOVEMBER 2013

THE PROBLEM WITH EXPONENTIAL GROWTH

THE PROBLEM WITH CANCER IS THE TUMOURS, and problems like tears in the lungs that don't tend to go away. They tend to get worse. I cannot believe quite how sick I have got in such a short space of time. I have officially had to move out of Boulcott and am definitely regressing back towards a baby state.

I have this awful cough, which makes me feel like my lungs want to be on the outside of my body rather than on the inside where they are supposed to be. I also can't eat much anymore, which also depletes the amount of energy I have. The painkillers make my mind a little more foggy. So yeah, I spend most of my days in bed!!

I have found this magical thing called Lonely (the Lonely Hearts bra range). They do these amazing bras that don't have underwire, so I can sleep in them and be comfortable. I am far more happy about this than I should be because I don't have to get undressed every time I hop into bed. You know you are getting sick when this is an achievement.

Then I have days like yesterday when I had a migraine, and instead of taking one day to fix itself, I am still feeling it a little bit. Which sucks. It must go away because tonight I am going to the One Republic concert with my friend Danielle.

When I used to say 'rest', I meant that I would not do much walking, but now I mean *rest.* I have not left the couch except to pee or shower. I am napping in full-on cat mode getting ready for tonight.

I'm lucky there have been loads of good things happening in my life, not just the fact that my friends from out of town have come back, or my friend Gilly has the most gorgeous puppy called Kelly!! Or the fact that my parents have agreed that I get to dog-sit a dog during the day!!! But that my friend, who I guess isn't my friend anymore, decided to ask me out!!!! This is super and ultra-exciting because I may have had a crush on him for quite a long time, and he's one of my best mates, so it was like — do I say anything? Luckily I didn't, coz he felt the same way :)

Oh right, his name is Mac, and he went to Wellington College and then did a gap year with Bex and everyone, so he lives in Wellington too. So that's all very exciting! Secretly, I really like this one. He's pretty awesome. Though, awkwardly, we don't have any pictures together — I will have to get some!

My friend Katie couldn't go to Taylor Swift so she gave me her two tickets. Guess who is getting a super-exciting date weekend in Auckland on the 29th? You do have my permission to feel sorry for him now, but I promise I'm not mean to him all the time, just a lot of it!

So my health isn't great and I don't know how much longer I have, but I still have many things which make me happy! ONE REPUBLIC TONIGHT!

ARE N'T I LUCKY?

Anthony and me at Brokeback Mountain.

Cuddles with Kelly.

TUESDAY, 10 DECEMBER 2013

PROJECT CUTE

I DON'T QUITE KNOW HOW TO START THIS BLOG POST as it has been so long since I did one. Well not really so long, but so much has happened. I should have written more but I was too sick or otherwise occupied, so I just wrote quick Facebook updates which seemed easier than trying to write a whole blog. This means that there is a big chunk of my story that is missing. So I guess this is me filling in all that has happened.

I ended up getting really sick. I mean *really* sick, so I had to go into hospital. I had pneumonia, and if anything was going to kill me that was it. Also my lungs were constantly filling up with fluid. It was so painful, and I must admit at one point I did wish I was not alive anymore. It hurt too much. It was a life that wasn't worth living.

I was left on IV antibiotics and told that I simply must get better. I think she must have sensed that I needed it, for little to my knowledge my friend Rebekah had been running around for weeks creating a video to remind me how much I am loved.

It could not have come at a better time. I was feeling beaten, like this was it. And my friends and family as always came through for me, showing how much they care, and were able to have many a laugh at my expense.

The video was screened at Queen Margaret's, and so many people helped out and put on an amazing spread. I literally hobbled quickly in, making a beeline for the nearest seat. I was soo sick, and sort of passed from one person's arms to the next pretending that I was keeping it together while struggling not to pass out from exhaustion and lack of oxygen.

That all changed.

I sat down, and could not help but laugh, cry and cringe with every minute of the video! It reminded me why I have to beat this pneumonia.

Thank you *so much*, Rebekah, and everyone who put so much effort into this film. I loved it in every single way.

CHECK IT OUT:
'PROJECT CUTE FOR HARRIET ROWLAND'
ON YOUTUBE.

Some of the beautiful
friends who came to movie night.

Mac (my boyfriend!! still not used
to calling him that!) & me.

Rebekah: the one girl
who made the whole
video. I could not ask
for a more amazing
friend. She is simply
spectacular.

WEDNESDAY, 11 DECEMBER 2013

SURVIVAL OF THE FITTEST

I CAN'T BELIEVE HOW QUICKLY TIME FLIES! Two weeks ago I went to the Taylor Swift concert in Auckland, thanks to the wonderful Katie who gave me her tickets. It was so much fun! I was coming out of the other side of my pneumonia, which was great, but I was still quite tired. I wasn't allowed to fly and I wasn't up to driving. Mac cannot drive, which I think is completely ridiculous. He maintains that it is a very normal thing. It's not.

So my mother and my brother kindly offered to drive us up. We stopped in Taupo on the way there and back, and spent two days in Auckland! I had such a wonderful time up there, and because we booked so late we ended up staying in SKYCITY!

It was so nice and really central. We arrived on the Friday afternoon, and I promptly did what I do best and had a nap. Then I woke up and demanded food, so Mac went down to Elliott Stables and got us some very yummy pizza. I sat on the hotel bed eating it and watching cartoons.

Mother and Father had suggested that I miss the opening act to conserve my energy, but it was seven o'clock, and I was ready and way too excited to sit still for a moment longer. So we jumped in a cab and went down to Vector Arena. I managed to see my friend Lucy while getting drinks, then do that silly wee dance you do while you sit down to the music of Neon Trees.

We had really good seats, but poor Mac felt a bit like a fish out of water as most of the audience were young girls (and some young boys) and their parents. Sadly, at 6'3 there is no way to hide him, but I think he felt better when this fabulously gay man came and sat next to us. He was in his early thirties and came by himself because none of his friends would go with him. He knew every word to every song. His smile alone made my night.

It was such a good concert. Taylor Swift had amazing dancers and her stage was one of the most amazing I have ever seen! I managed to do some awesome chair grooving. (I stood for a few songs but ran out of breath pretty quickly.)

I spent all of Saturday seeing my friends in Auckland. I met up with Claudia for brunch — we went to Depot which is the Al Brown restaurant! It was so delicious, and it's always awesome seeing Clauds. I spent the whole afternoon down in Britomart with some of my amazing friends from Boulcott — two of them had driven up from Hamilton to see me.

After that, I had a rest back at the hotel until my friend Josh came. He has been in the Navy for the last couple of months in training to become an officer. He graduated and got a leadership award, and I could not be prouder of this amazing man. He is a seriously wonderful boy! I went out for dinner with him. I even had time for a drink with Chloe, Alex and Bex who were up in Auckland for the concert too.

I was so proud of how much I was able to do. My friends really do mean the world to me, and to be able to see them and catch up was awesome!

It was an amazing weekend, and really nice considering how sick I'd been. It showed me how much better I am. After spending two weeks bedridden it was a relief to have a change of scenery, and see people who are important to me that I never thought I'd see again.

IT'S STRANGE THE THINGS
LIFE THROWS IN YOUR FACE,
THE GOOD AND THE BAD,
AND THIS WEEKEND WAS
SUCH A GOOD TIME!!!

We had such amazing seats.

Lunch with Claudia at Depot.

Cheeky selfie before the show.

Some of my wonderful
from Boulcott.

SUNDAY, 15 DECEMBER 2013

HOW TO HAVE FUN WITHOUT A DOG

IF YOU DON'T KNOW THIS ABOUT ME, I would probably say you don't know me very well. I am not very good at sitting still, EVER really. But sometimes my body dictates, especially now with this whole cancer thing, that I must lie down.

Luckily the rest that is forced on my body is made better by having people to visit! It's literally been so wonderful — so many friends have been spending such a huge time out in Paremata Road. My friend Jess flew up to see me.

Luckily, this week I have had awesome events to distract me too. Philippa Boyens is honestly one of the kindest people I know — she is so busy yet finds time to fit me in. She came to visit me in hospital with Fran Walsh and Katie Jackson before they ran off to premiere *The Hobbit* in LA. I was also invited to the New Zealand premiere with my friend Tessa (who was up again from Christchurch to see me). We had the most wonderful night dressing up with the help of Sophie and Zoe. It was such a fun night and the movie is honestly so good. If anyone is tossing up going, just go. It's awesome!

The whole *Hobbit* cast has been so good to me. Richard Armitage wrote me an email which said, 'You are such a wonderful, funny, thoughtful, smart, brave girl.' I must admit this made my day that much better. He is such an amazing person not only to think of me while busily promoting a movie, but to write me an email!

The very next day after *The Hobbit* premiere, I went to the Governor General's house for their Christmas party. It is such a pretty place. Kate, Finn and Finn's mum Amanda got to meet the Governor General and his wife and son!

I remember saying at the beginning of this blog that my life is surreal, and judging by the last two days, it kind of is. My mother is worried I will turn into a Wellington socialite, without realising that I already am. It's always a hard question when people say to me, 'What do you do?' The simplest and most truthful reply would be, 'I have fun'. These past two days, that *is* what I've done.

I HAVE HAD TWO OF THE BEST DAYS
OF MY LIFE, EVEN WITHOUT A DOG!

My awesome mother & father
sending me off to *The Hobbit*.

Zoe & Sophie who helped
the lovely Tessa & me get ready.

Tessa & me, red-carpet ready.

Kate & me.

Kate & me outside the Governor General's house.

AHHHHHH! It's about to start!

LAST POST

I GUESS THIS IS IT, THE END OF MY STORY. I know what is going to happen, yet somehow I don't. Life throws you a curve ball now and then, so I may have some adventures yet. I know I am going to die, and I know it will be sooner rather than later. I wish it wasn't true, and it wasn't going to happen, but it is.

One of my favourite quotes from *The Fault in Our Stars* is 'some infinities are bigger than other infinities', and it just happens to be that mine is smaller than most, but that does not mean I have been unlucky. I think I have been terribly lucky in my life. There are the places I have gone and the people who decided to let me be their friend. I even fell in love not just once but twice with two incredible guys, at different times of course — what kind of girl do you think I am? Lastly, I have one of the most incredible families on this earth. I have had a wonderful and amazing life.

My life has been one long adventure, but at sometime or another all journeys must come to an end. I live at a million miles an hour, trying to squeeze as much as I can into every day. Death, for me, will be a